THE STEAM A
GASLIGHT

Travelling by Train in Late Victorian London
1871–1900

Peter Hodge

Published by

MELROSE BOOKS

An Imprint of Melrose Press Limited
St Thomas Place, Ely
Cambridgeshire
CB7 4GG, UK
www.melrosebooks.com

FIRST EDITION

Cover designed by Peter Hodge
Cover image: Ludgate Hill, London, by Wilhelm Trübner

ISBN 978-1-907040-16-0

Printed in Great Britain by:
The MPG Books Group
Bodmin and King's Lynn

© **Mixed Sources**

Product group from well-managed
forests, controlled sources and
recycled wood or fiber
www.fsc.org Cert no. TT-COC-002303
© 1996 Forest Stewardship Council

FSC

DEDICATION

In memory of Andrew,
with whom I shared much railway humour.

Snow falls in the buffet of Aldersgate station,
Toiling and doomed from Moorgate Street puffs the train,
For us of the steam and the gas-light, the lost generation,
The new white cliffs of the City are built in vain.

John Betjeman

THE MAIDEN'S PRAYER
A sketch at Aldersgate Street Station

CONTENTS

ABBREVIATIONS

GER	Great Eastern Railway
GNR	Great Northern Railway
GWR	Great Western Railway
LBSCR	London, Brighton and South Coast Railway
LCDR	London, Chatham and Dover Railway
LNWR	London and North Western Railway
LSWR	London and South Western Railway
LTSR	London, Tilbury and Southend Railway
MDR	Metropolitan District Railway (the "District")
Met	Metropolitan Railway
MR	Midland Railway
NLR	North London Railway
SER	South Eastern Railway

The titles of newspapers and periodicals most frequently referred to are abbreviated in the notes as follows:

BST	Brixton & Streatham Times
HFPJ	Hornsey & Finsbury Park Journal
IG	Islington Gazette
RFS	Railway Fly Sheet (& Official Gazette from 1875)
ROG	Railway Official Gazette
RSOG	Railway Sheet & Official Gazette
RTT	Richmond & Twickenham Times
SLP	South London Press

The following books referred to in the notes are identified there by the author's surname:

Barker T & Robbins M, *A History of London Transport,* Vol. 1 (1963)
Course E, *London Railways* (1962)

Dickens C, *Dictionary of London* (1888)

Emmerson A, *The Underground Pioneers* (2000)

Hyde R, *Printed Maps of Victorian London* (1975)

Kellett J, *Railways and Victorian Cities* (1969)

Lee C, *The Metropolitan District Railway* (1956)

Nock O, *The Great Northern Railway* (1958)

Robbins M, *The North London Railway* (1974)

Sekon G, *Locomotion in Victorian London* (1938)

Walford E, *Old and New London* (1872–78), Vol. 5

White H, *A Regional History of the Railways of Great Britain*, Vol. 3, *Greater London* (1963)

Young J, *Great Northern Suburban* (1977)

Other titles are given in full in the notes. *RFS* became *RSOG* in 1877 and *ROG* in 1882.

Gustave Doré: *Over London – By Rail*, c. 1870

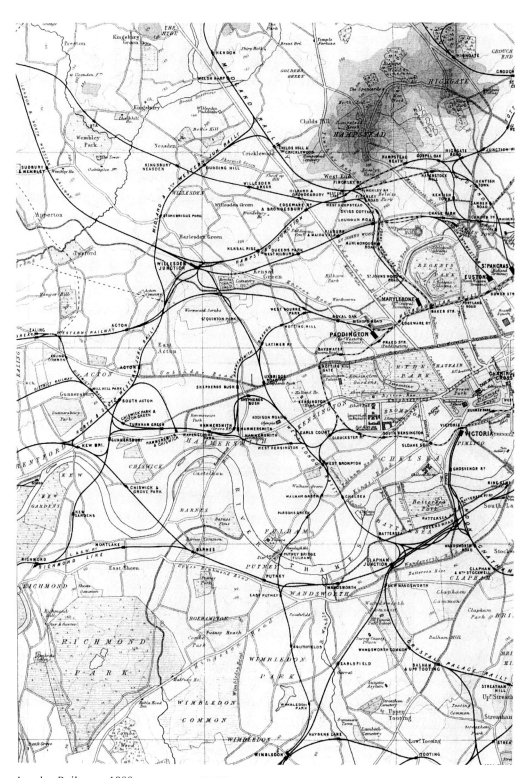

London Railways, 1899

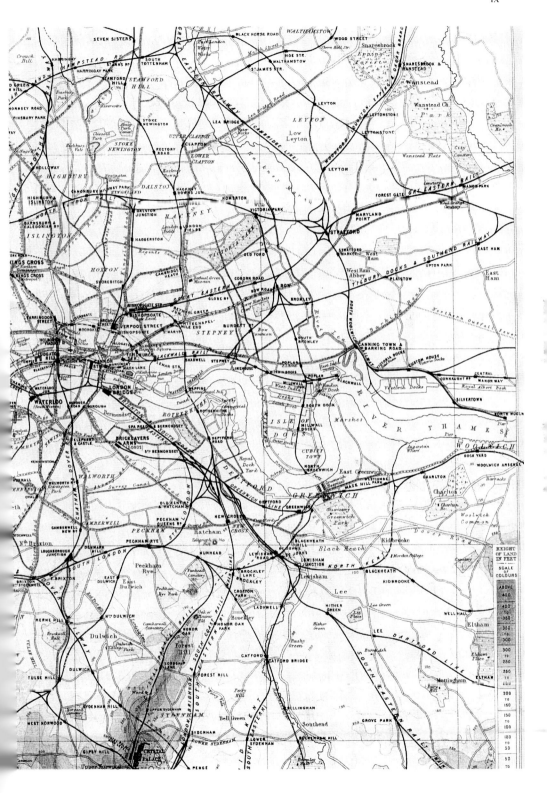

INTRODUCTION

Much has been written about the planning, construction and operation of London's railways, but rather less about the passenger's experience of using them. This book aims to tilt the balance a little by looking at train travel in late Victorian London from the user's point of view.

Most of the surface and sub-surface railways laid down in London by 1900 still exist, but the services provided over them have changed greatly. The range and complexity of steam passenger services operated in the late Victorian period were remarkable. It is with the user's response to this tangled web of train services that this book is concerned.

No rigid geographical boundaries have been set, but the bulk of the content relates to journeys within an area of London that by 1900 had become continuously built up. Most of the passengers whose travel experiences are reported were therefore residents of London and its expanding suburbs. There is a broad definition of the area in Chapter One.

The book opens with a brief overview of late Victorian London and its railways. Characteristics of the train services, printed information about them and fares charged to use them are considered. The passenger's experience at stations and on trains is explored, and some examples of travel hazards are given. The book concludes with a few eye-witness accounts of journeys undertaken.

Much of the evidence from rail users is anecdotal, consisting as it must do of individual experiences and subjective impressions. Since users of any public service tend to remain silent when they are satisfied and to complain when they are not, there is an inevitable bias towards adverse criticism. Nonetheless, praise is sometimes forthcoming, and is given due weight when it is offered. In the belief that users should be allowed to speak for themselves, verbatim reporting of written comments is employed wherever this seems the best way of representing the writer's thoughts and feelings.

The reported experiences of passengers, and their comments, criticisms and suggestions, are drawn chiefly from contemporary newspapers and periodicals – especially London local newspapers. The latter have proved to be a rich source of material, and whilst due allowance must be made for journalistic exaggeration, many of the issues raised occur repeatedly and were clearly of real concern.

* * *

Even to those who did not use them, railways in late Victorian London were inescapable. Gustave Doré's well-known c.1870 engraving of brick viaducts towering over rows of grim terraced houses and their backyards illustrates dramatically the railways' visual impact. But one should not forget the associated noise – the barking of locomotive exhausts, the hiss of escaping steam, the shriek of engine whistles, the clattering over points and crossings, the squealing of wheels on curves, the banging of compartment doors, and the raucous attempts of platform porters to make themselves heard above this cacophony. Where shunting was performed, the ringing of steel on steel would frequently be heard. In foggy weather (and winter fogs, or "London Particulars", occurred often), the loud report of fog detonators, placed on the line at the approach to signals, would fill the air. Railway noises were but a part of the medley of sounds heard in late Victorian London, but a significant part wherever the railways had a strong presence.

To some observers, the sights and sounds of the railways were impressive – even sublime. A writer on "Artists and Railways" affirmed in 1889 that "the sight of trains entering and leaving an underground metropolitan station is, to a man of perceptive nature, calculated to touch those feelings which art labours so assiduously, and often so vainly, to affect".[1] Four years later another writer likened the interior of St. Pancras Station to an old Egyptian temple, "dimly visible through the veil of Isis, though we call it London fog":

> *The white clouds come from the altar fire; above it, half lost in vapour, is*
> *the great clock, its huge round dial like the face of a monstrous idol before*
> *which burn in solemn stillness the hanging lamps, gleaming silver and*
> *violet and rose.*[2]

Few of the late Victorian railway travellers whose voices we shall hear in the following pages would have been moved by such soul-stirring sights. A safe and comfortable journey in a clean and punctual train would have been their keenest desire.

---

1. *Cassell's Family Magazine*, Dec. 1889, quoted in *ROG*, Dec. 1889.
2. *English Illustrated Magazine*, June 1893, reprinted in *Railway Magazine*, July–Aug. 1944.

ACKNOWLEDGEMENTS

The British Library Newspaper Library at Colindale was the source of most of the newspapers and periodicals consulted; thanks are due to the staff of the library for their assistance in the use of the collection.

The cover illustration is reproduced by permission of the Fine Art Photographic Library.

The verse from John Betjeman's poem *Monody on the Death of Aldersgate Street Station*, from his *Collected Poems*, is reproduced by permission of John Murray (Publishers).

The cartoons on pages iv, 27, 30, 41, 60, 65, 72, 76, 84 and 93 are from *Punch Library of Humour: Mr. Punch's Railway Book* (The Educational Book Co., c. 1900).

The London railway map (pages viii and ix) is from George Newnes's *Royal Atlas of England and Wales* (1899).

The engraving on page vii is from Blanchard Jerrold & Gustave Doré, *London: A Pilgrimage* (Grant & Co., 1872) and is reproduced by permission of the Museum of London.

The timetable on page 4 is from the *Railway Fly Sheet*, July 1871, and is reproduced by permission of the British Library.

The engravings on pages 7, 28 and 29 are from the *Illustrated London News,* 30.9.1865, 22.4.1865, 10.6.1865 and 3.2.1866 and respectively.

The drawings by William Heath Robinson on pages 35, 68 and 86 are from W. Heath Robinson, *Railway Ribaldry* (Great Western Railway, 1935) and are reproduced by permission of Pollinger Limited and the proprietor.

The cartoons on pages 44, 47 and 53 are from the *South London Press* (4.5.1889, 22.6.1889 and 29.6.1889 respectively) and are reproduced by permission of the British Library.

All other illustrations are from the author's collection.

CHAPTER 1

LATE VICTORIAN LONDON
AND ITS RAILWAYS

To Work from the Suburbs

By the middle of the nineteenth century London had become a major commercial and financial centre. This development was accompanied by a massive growth in population, which increased sixfold through the century to reach 6.6 million by 1900. At the same time, the resident population of central London declined, as businesses, roads and railways supplanted private dwellings.

The population growth could be accommodated only by outward expansion. Many people who had previously lived close to or on top of their work now needed transport to carry them daily between home and employment. From the mid-nineteenth century, the railways increasingly met this need by providing relatively cheap and fast travel between the growing suburbs and the central business districts. This enabled many workers to live in cleaner, healthier and more pleasant surroundings. As working hours shortened and incomes rose, more and more employees were able to travel daily between suburb and town.[1]

Growth of the new suburbs depended not only on the provision of efficient transport, but also on the availability of affordable housing. Speculative builders were not slow to recognise the financial rewards to be gained from covering green fields with bricks and mortar. Often they would begin by erecting a small housing development close to a railway station as an impetus to further growth in the area. Typically a suburb would then grow outwards, eventually merging with other suburbs whose development had started in the same way. Thus would begin the process of suburban sprawl that characterised late Victorian London.[2]

The process was greeted with dismay by some suburban residents who witnessed the disappearance of countryside once on their doorstep. "Rural beauty is fast fading away in many parts of South London", wrote a commentator in 1872. "That quiet-looking and pleasant old walk from South-east Brixton to Herne Hill, which was always a favourite with

---

1. Barker & Robbins pp. xxv–xxvii
2. Trent C, *Greater London* (1965) pp. 191–192, 204–205

me, has been thrown over to the care of the navvy and the hod-carrier." The writer observed that, although much of the newly built property remained unlet, preparations were in hand for the erection of 500 more houses in the neighbourhood. "In a few years Herne Hill will have been absorbed into the thickly populated town."[3]

At first it was the burgeoning middle classes who could afford to populate the new suburbs. The rows of terraced or semi-detached villas in which many of them lived may have looked monotonous, but they were a vast improvement on the inner-city deprivation suffered by earlier generations. The new suburbs were bastions of middle class respectability, shielded from the incursions of the lower orders by the level of house prices and rents and the cost of season tickets.

Less desirable were the many working class suburbs that developed rapidly after 1870 in response to the provision of cheap rail fares and workmen's trains. They were populated by unskilled workers, artisans and clerks. Most of the houses were in dull, standardised terraces with small gardens, and development was dense. Streets were often laid out in unimaginative grid patterns, and trees were scarce. Working class suburbs predominated in north-east and south-east London.

The geographical spread of suburbs around London was uneven, depending on the presence of railways, the quality of train service, and the availability of cheap fares. Broadly speaking, however, the continuously built-up area of suburban London extended about eight miles from Charing Cross by 1900. Beyond that there were significant centres of population separated from the sprawl by open country but nevertheless contributing to the daily flow of travellers to and from work in central London. Continuous building spread as far as Ealing in the west, New Barnet and Edmonton in the north, Ilford in the east and Croydon in the south. Suburban centres as yet detached from the continuous building included Wembley, Enfield, Barking and Sutton.[4]

Leisure and Pleasure

The increased mobility afforded by the railways in late Victorian London also encouraged the growth of leisure activities. Entertainments, exhibitions, museums, galleries and sporting events grew in number and popularity as the century progressed. The Bank Holiday Acts of 1871 and 1875 established new public holidays on Easter Monday, Whit Monday, the first Monday in August and Boxing Day. These, especially in the spring and summer, created a massive demand for excursion traffic by rail.[5]

Foremost among the attractions was the Crystal Palace, removed to Sydenham in 1854 after closure of the 1851 Great Exhibition in Hyde Park. It proved to be a great success in its new location, attracting millions of visitors. "Throughout the whole of the world there is no place of amusement that can equal the Palace", claimed a journalist in 1885. "Its capabilities

---

3.   *SLP* 13.1.1872
4.   Jackson A, *Semi-Detached London* (1973) pp. 21–23
5.   Barker & Robbins pp. 203–204

are enormous. They have been tested to the utmost and never been found to fail."[6] But by the late 1880s the palace was facing competition from other attractions. In 1887 a correspondent in the *Times* even referred to the "failure" of the palace, and offered suggestions as to how it could be made more attractive to the visitor.[7]

North London's answer to the Crystal Palace was the Alexandra Palace. The idea had its origins in the 1851 exhibition, but the project was beset with financial difficulties. The palace that was eventually opened on 24th May 1873 was smaller than its south London rival and not chiefly of glass, but a contemporary observer commented that "it may challenge comparison [with Crystal Palace] for its picturesque appearance, and in natural advantages the site of the new palace is infinitely superior".[8] The sun-filled optimism of the opening day, however, was soon to give way to disaster when, on 9th June 1873, fire reduced the palace to a charred and gutted shell. Rebuilding progressed with commendable speed, and the new palace was opened on 1st May 1875.[9] It enjoyed some years of success, but in the later nineteenth century faced even more acute financial difficulties than its south London counterpart.

For Londoners intent on enjoying country pleasures, railways provided access to parkland, green fields and forest within or close to the metropolis. By the early 1870s Epping Forest had become a favourite destination for East Enders on public holidays. In 1878 the future of the forest was secured when it was acquired by the Corporation of London, and on 6th May 1882 Queen Victoria travelled by special train from Windsor to Chingford via Acton and Stratford to declare the forest free for "the use and enjoyment of the public for all time".[10] However, she would not have been amused by the claim that Epping Forest was "where the riff-raff of the East End congregate on Bank Holidays" and where the visitor "will see the festive coster in all the beauty of his war-paint, and in exuberant spirits – liquid and otherwise".[11]

Closer to central London, but no less popular as a pleasure resort, was Hampstead Heath, declared a public open space in 1871. The Bank Holiday entertainments there always drew large crowds; on Easter Monday 1895, for example, they had "a very animated and fair-like appearance, with the hosts of cocoa-nut shies, peep-shows, exhibitions, refreshment stalls... ice barrows, try-your-weight chairs, phonographs, conjurors, &c." – not to mention the swing-boats and steam roundabout near the Vale of Health tea-gardens, or the bladders fixed to the ends of sticks that "furnished the means for much good humoured mimic warfare. ...The whole day was one of great enjoyment to myriads of London's toilers".[12] Without the railways, the opportunity for such enjoyment would have been denied to many.

---

6. *Norwood News* 7.2.1885
7. *Times* 19.2.1887
8. *IG* 27.5.1873
9. Goode C, *Ally Pally* (1983) pp. 19–27
10. *Times* 6.5.1882
11. *East London Advertiser* 5.8.1893
12. *Hampstead & Highgate Express* 20.4.1895

MIDLAND RAILWAY.

TIME TABLE OF TRAINS BETWEEN LONDON AND WELSH HARP AND ELSTREE.—JULY, 1871.

	a m	a m	a m A	a m	a m A	a m	a m	noon	p m	p m	p m B	p m	p m A	p m	p m A	p m	p m	p m	p m	p m A	p m	p m	p m
Moorgate Street ... dep.	...	8 5	8 53	9 54	10 7	10 20	10 50	12 23	1 32	2 10	3 14	3 20	4 2	4 25	5 0	5 28	6 7	6 20	7 20	8 49	9 4		
St. Pancras ... ,,	6 20	8 5	9 6	...	10 20	...	...	...	1 35	...	3 25	3 20	4 10	4 37	...	5 45	...	6 25	...	...	9 25		
Kentish Town ... ,,	6 28	8 20	9 12	10 9	10 26	10 35	11 5	12 38	1 50	2 25	3 32	3 35	4 22	4 43	5 15	5 53	6 22	6 38	7 35	9 4	9 31		
Welsh Harp ... ... arr.	...	8 35	9 27	10 26	...	10 52	11 22	12 55	2 7	2 42	3 49	52	...	...	5 32	...	6 39	...	7 52	9 22	...		
Elstree & Boreham Wood ,,	7 0	...	9 45	...	10 52	...	...	...	2 25	...	4 7	...	4 54	5 7	...	6 25	...	7 12	...	...	10 3		

	a m	a m	a m A	a m	a m	noon	p m	p m	p m	p m	p m	p m	p m A	p m	p m	p m	p m	p m	p m	p m	p m
Elstree & Boreham Wood dep.	8 2	...	8 53	10 3	...	12 10	...	...	2 40	...	...	4 57	5 32	...	...	7 1	...	...	...	...	...
Welsh Harp ... ... ,,	...	8 46	...	...	10 40	12 26	12 34	1 18	2 56	3 34	4 31	5 14	...	5 59	6 50	7 18	8 3	9 51	...	...	...
Kentish Town ... arr.	8 31	9 3	9 26	10 30	10 57	12 44	12 50	1 35	3 12	3 51	4 48	5 32	6 4	6 15	7 7	7 39	8 20	10 8	...	...	...
St. Pancras ... ,,	8 35	...	9 30	10 35	...	12 50	...	1 55	3 18	...	...	5 38	6 10	...	...	7 45	...	...	...	...	...
Moorgate Street ... ,,	8 48	9 18	9 44	10 47	11 12	1 5	1 5	1 50	3 39	4 6	5 3	5 51	6 30	6 30	7 22	8 9	8 35	10 23	...	...	...

Trains marked A are First and Second Class; all others are First, Second, and Third.   Train marked B runs on Saturdays only.

Derby, July, 1871.   JAMES ALLPORT, General Manager.

Printed for the Proprietor by M'Corquodale & Co.'s, Cardington Street, London, N.W.

The Midland Railway train service between London, Welsh Harp and Elstree in July 1871. Welsh Harp Station was opened in 1870 and became a popular summer destination for anglers and ornithologists visiting the Welsh Harp Reservoir, then known as Kingsbury Lake. The reservoir was well stocked with fish and frequented by many species of birds. Other attractions were boating, lakeside tea gardens and a nearby racecourse. The latter was closed in the late 1870s after becoming notorious for dishonest dealing and bad behaviour.

Railways and Reputations

Within the area outlined above, the rail network was well-established by 1871. To the west and north of London the GWR, LNWR and GNR main lines from Paddington, Euston and King's Cross respectively had been open for some years, and the MR from St. Pancras since 1868. Away from the main lines, suburban branches were beginning to fill the gaps. To the north-east and east of London, the GER termini at Bishopsgate and Fenchurch Street served three main lines and a few branches. Within inner north London, the NLR and LNWR operated from their City terminus at Broad Street. Although the Inner Circle had yet to be completed by the Met and MDR, the Met had already opened the first section of its extension line, from Baker Street to Swiss Cottage.

To the south of London, the network was even more developed by 1871. The LSWR main line from Waterloo had sprouted several suburban branches, whilst the LBSCR network from Victoria and London Bridge to south London was almost complete. The LCDR, with its cross-river links from Victoria and Ludgate Hill, was also well-established. During the

1860s the SER had secured termini north of the Thames, at Charing Cross and Cannon Street, from which it served the growing suburbs of south-east London.

The period under review saw the construction of about fifty significant new lines or sections of line. Given the very wide coverage south of the Thames by 1871, it is not surprising that more than three quarters of the new lines opening to passenger traffic in the ensuing thirty years were north of the river. During the first half of the 1870s new lines in London were opening at the rate of about four a year. During the late 1870s and into the 1880s new openings dwindled to an average of about two a year. From 1890 to the turn of the century they were an occasional occurrence.

By the mid 1880s, the 13 railway companies providing local train services in London together served about 300 stations, of which about 45 per cent were on main lines and their branches north of the Thames, 30 per cent on main lines and their branches south of the Thames, 20 per cent on the underground lines and their extensions, and 5 per cent on jointly managed orbital routes.[13]

"How is it that the southern Railway Companies are so mean in their relations to the public in comparison with the northern lines?" asked a commentator in 1881.[14] There seems to have been a general presumption that railway passengers fared better north than south of the Thames, and that the southern companies failed to keep pace with residential development, either through financial caution or sheer inertia. This press comment is from 1883:

> London, ever increasing London, is growing daily, stretching out its arms more and more, especially towards the south. ...The builder goes on merrily, not giving a thought to the means of getting to and from the great centre of business. That is no concern of his, and the Railway Companies are slow to move. ...Let the Railway Company be once convinced that a more liberal policy will bring increased profit, and sooner or later they will make an effort to reap the harvest which is only waiting to be gathered in.[15]

Attitudes to the south London companies may have been coloured by the almost universally bad press received by the LCDR, whose passengers complained vigorously throughout the late Victorian period. In April 1877 a well-attended meeting of LCDR passengers took place at Peckham Rye to protest against the "unjust, unfair, and irregular proceedings of the company in their conduct towards their passengers". Late and overcrowded trains seem to have been the main cause of complaint. "The time had come when the public... should assert its position and show the company that they were not the masters, but the servants."[16]

---

13. For the development of London's railways see White H, *A Regional History of the Railways of Great Britain*, Vol.3, *Greater London* (1963)
14. *SLP* 12.2.1881
15. *SLP* 21.7.1883
16. *Camberwell News* 14.4.1877

Allegations of mismanagement continued. In June 1889 another crowded meeting at Peckham produced "ample evidence that the patience of the long-suffering passengers has now reached its limit". The company had turned a deaf ear to passengers' complaints, and had refused to meet deputations: "in all respects the LCDR is the worst-managed line which has had metropolitan and suburban powers conferred upon it".[17] And so it seems to have remained until 1899, when its effective amalgamation with the SER under a joint management committee to form the South Eastern and Chatham Railway brought hope of a better future.

It is harder to find sustained criticism of any of the railway companies north of the Thames. The directors of the NLR, and its big brother the LNWR, must have been gratified by the quite frequent plaudits of their performance. Writing in 1873 in support of the NLR, a correspondent said "I think the company is entitled to great praise for the efficiency with which their enormous traffic is conducted, and the civility and attention of their employees".[18] Just over twenty years later, a columnist wrote:

> I have frequently admired the London and North Western Railway. The punctuality of its trains, and their comfort and good "get up", the smoothness with which the trains run, the unswerving politeness of the officials, are all matters for admiration on the part of the passenger and envy on that of rival lines.[19]

Of all the railway companies in London, the GER received the most consistent and lavish praise. By the early 1890s it had earned a reputation as the most punctual railway in England, and was setting an example for others to follow in its response to increasing residential traffic. Prompted by a visit to the growing Bush Hill Park estate, near Enfield, in 1891, a reporter penned this accolade:

> It could scarcely have been conceived, ten years ago, that the Great Eastern Railway would have been called upon to bring so many tens of thousands daily into London, and take them back again to their suburban homes. This obligation, however, has come, and is being every week intensified, and a large meed of praise is due to the Great Eastern Railway for the energy, determination and promptitude, to say nothing of the extended liberality with which they have combated the increasing difficulties surrounding the discharge of this all important cumulative responsibility.[20]

---

17. *SLP* 22.6.1889
18. *IG* 20.5.1873
19. *Kilburn Times* 23.11.1894
20. *Tottenham & Edmonton Weekly Herald* 7.8.1891

In 1893 the GER was considered to stand "amongst the first in the ranks of railway progress" and to be "one of the most powerful companies of the future".[21]

Generally favourable public attitudes towards railway companies could of course mask detailed and specific complaints. As we explore the experiences and concerns of London's late Victorian rail travellers, numerous causes of dissatisfaction will emerge. But the shortcomings should be seen in the context of what the railways were providing – the most extensive and elaborate network of urban and suburban steam passenger train services of any capital city.

Crystal Palace High Level Station.

Despite its reputation for weak management, the LCDR responded ambitiously to the opportunity for attracting new traffic to the Crystal Palace. The High Level station was opened by the LCDR on 1st August 1865 as the terminus of a new line from Peckham Rye. The spacious, wholly enclosed station was an exuberant specimen of Victorian architecture, designed to handle the vast crowds of pleasure seekers visiting the adjacent palace. With a direct subway connection, the High Level station gave better access to the palace than the rival Low Level station of the LBSCR, opened in 1856.

21.   *East London Advertiser* 20.5.1893, 5.8.1893

CHAPTER 2
LOCAL RAIL SERVICES AND THEIR USERS

A Tangled Web

A country clergyman, unfamiliar with the ways of the metropolis, let alone the complications of its railways, came up to London for a church meeting in May 1872. Having occasion to travel on the SER between London Bridge and Charing Cross, he was astonished to observe that, in the course of the journey, he crossed the Thames three times. To get to the other side of a river by crossing it thrice was a new experience, and he wondered whether he had been mistaken. To be quite sure, therefore, he decided to take a train back to London Bridge. To his amazement the journey was accomplished with one crossing of the river. Fearing for his sanity, he bought another ticket to return to Charing Cross, and to his utter bewilderment the train crossed the river three times. "It's no use", he muttered, hopelessly. "I must give it up." And so he did, reflecting on "the inscrutable mysteries of railroads".[1]

A true story? So it is claimed, though the reverend gentleman's failure to remark that the train called at Cannon Street in one direction is surprising. However, the tale does hint amusingly at the pitfalls facing the user of London's late Victorian railway system. Its complexities were addressed in more general terms by another writer in the same year:

> To the mathematical mind the study of a London railway map may possibly be extremely interesting; but to ordinary persons the attempt to unravel its ramifications is something excruciating. At the present time it is just as easy to follow the lines which cross and recross one another over the metropolis, as it would be to trace the threads in a spider's web, so manifold and intricate are they. Go into any railway station and ask to be booked to the first place you may think of, and the chances are that they will oblige you, although you may consider yourself under the special protection of an overruling Providence if you ever reach your destination, for at every junction, and their number is legion, you run the risk of being whirled away in quite the opposite direction to that in which you desire to be conveyed.[2]

---

1. *SLP* 18.5.1872
2. *SLP* 3.8.1872

Sixteen years later Charles Dickens (son of the novelist), in his *Dictionary of London*, marvelled at the skill and ingenuity expended to create "the labyrinth of stations, junctions, tunnels, viaducts, embankments, and cuttings, running in such quick succession", but had sympathy with the traveller "who wants to understand the extraordinary ramifications of the interior railway system of London. Looked at from the point of view of the timetables, such a journey as that from Old Kent Road to Willesden, or from Kew Bridge to Dalston, is not to be contemplated without dismay".[3]

Examination of timetables of the period confirms that journey planning could indeed have been a real challenge. To begin with, service frequencies, and therefore interchange times, varied enormously. On common sections of route traversed by several services, trains could be running a few minutes apart. On the other hand, some individual point-to-point services might consist of only a handful of trains a day. Between these two extremes were many services which, though offering a reasonable number of trains throughout the day, did so in an apparently random fashion with irregular intervals between trains and wide gaps in service at certain times.

Take, for example, the weekday service between Peckham Rye and Ludgate Hill, about which representations were made to the LCDR in February 1890. During the morning business period intervals of up to thirty minutes occurred between trains, whereas in a quieter period between 10.28 and 10.45 in the morning there were no fewer than three trains to the City. Passengers returning to Peckham in the early evening faced intervals of up to forty-four minutes. At Saturday lunch-time (a busy period for home-going office workers) there was a thirty-four minute gap in the service. Dissatisfied users prepared a "memorial" to the company: "We cannot think", they said "that the train service is as frequent or convenient as it should be on what is really a metropolitan line".[4]

Some companies did provide even-interval services from an early date. The NLR, for example, ran trains at fifteen-minute intervals on each of the main legs of its network. The Met and MDR, operating at high frequencies on the Inner Circle, needed regularity of service to maximise capacity. From 1889 a daytime service of nineteen trains an hour in each direction ran between Gloucester Road and Mansion House – an impressive frequency for steam-hauled trains of slam-door compartment stock. Four of these trains per hour operated on the Middle and Outer Circle services, both introduced in 1872 and each running on a half-hourly frequency.[5]

The Middle Circle, provided by the GWR, ran from Moorgate Street (later from Aldgate) to Mansion House via Bishop's Road, Latimer Road, Addison Road and Earl's Court. The Outer Circle, provided by the LNWR, ran from Broad Street to Mansion House via Hampstead, Willesden, Addison Road and Earl's Court. They were examples of the once numerous local steam suburban services that followed circuitous routes around the capital in the late Victorian period, providing interchange opportunities with radial lines. Their commencement in 1872 was welcomed as a valuable addition to the London railway system:

---

3.   Dickens pp. 157, 209
4.   *SLP* 15.2.1890
5.   Lee p. 29

As the saving of time is of the utmost importance, the businessman hails
with great satisfaction these increased facilities; and it is impossible to
overrate the advantages which passengers from all parts of the country
derive from the principal railway lines being connected.[6]

On circuitous routes such as these, with trains calling at many, closely spaced stations, average speeds were unavoidably low. As most of the traffic was relatively short distance, however, low speeds mattered less than on radial suburban routes into London. But with steam traction, slow braking and acceleration, and mechanical signalling, journey times on some of the radial routes were equally unimpressive. There was continual pressure from users for faster suburban journeys throughout the late Victorian period.

In 1885 residents of Norwood, Anerley and Sydenham protested to the LBSCR about the slowness of their train service to Victoria. Stopping trains from Norwood to Victoria via Crystal Palace took up to three quarters of an hour to complete the ten-mile journey. Unfavourable comparisons were made with railways in north London, and it was argued that residential property could not be let because of the inferior train service. The "beautiful suburbs" of Norwood and Sydenham were in decline, it was said, and a resident of Anerley wrote: "It is indeed deplorable to see such a pretty and healthy neighbourhood deserted simply because the railway company... are not alive to their own interests". The residents wanted fast trains from Norwood to Victoria calling only at Clapham Junction, which they said would bring Norwood as close to the West End as West Kensington was.[7]

Discontent was also aired from time to time over the absence of very early morning and late night services on some lines. Cheap early morning trains for workmen were a common feature of weekday timetables, but services in the small hours of the morning were a rarity. In 1897 the MR was asked to run a very early morning train to stations on the South Tottenham line for the benefit of newspaper employees who finished work well after midnight and had to wait for the first morning train back to the suburbs. Nearly 300 "press" workers, it was claimed, would use an early train. The MR met the request with a train from St. Pancras at 3.45 a.m., but a petition to the GNR for a similar train from King's Cross was rejected.[8]

Late night service provision was variable. Complaints were made from time to time of "early" finishing times on services with last trains already running well after 11 p.m. – an indication that late night services were widely expected. During the 1870s trains on the Inner Circle ran up to midnight, but withdrawal of the midnight train from Mansion House in 1872 attracted some sarcastic press comment. The MDR, apparently without notice, had brought forward the time of the last train to 11.40 p.m., "with a delicate attention to the interests of its customers". Theatre-goers returning home late were evidently taken by surprise, and had to secure cabs or walk home, as "no staring placards have defaced the stations apprising the public of the nature of the boon".[9]

On some suburban routes services ran beyond midnight. By 1898, for example, the last

6.   *SLP* 3.8.1872
7.   *Norwood News* 10.1.1885, 21.11.1885
8.   *HFPJ* 6.2.1897, *Tottenham & Edmonton Weekly Herald* 16.8.1901
9.   *SLP* 23.11.1872

LSWR suburban train was leaving Waterloo at 12.20 a.m., but from 1st July of that year the company went even further and introduced two later trains from Waterloo to Clapham Junction at 12.40 and 1 a.m., benefiting "a considerable number of people employed in connection with theatres, restaurants, and hotels".[10] A year earlier, the GER had introduced a half-hourly all-night service between Liverpool Street and Wood Street (Walthamstow), considered at the time to be a bold initiative.[11]

Late Victorian attitudes to Sunday observance were reflected in a generally low level of train service provision on that day, and an almost complete absence of trains during the two-hour "church interval" from 11 a.m. to 1 p.m. In theory, the main purpose of the break was to enable railway employees to attend church, but few did so, and they would in any case have been out of place in their uniforms or working clothes. A survey on the Met in 1876 revealed little use of Sunday morning trains, and the "church interval" continued on the Inner Circle until 1900. It survived on the NLR as late as 1921.[12]

Whilst the "church interval" seems to have been accepted as part of the Victorian way of life, the limited Sunday services available outside church hours did attract some criticism. In 1897, for example, the GNR and MR were taken to task for the inadequate pre-church service from the neighbouring Stroud Green and Crouch Hill Stations respectively to Moorgate Street. The GNR offered departures at 8.24 and 9.56, the MR at 8.26 and 9.50 – both either too early or too late to make good onward connections. "This seems a glorious illustration of the way not to do it", moaned a complainant. "However disinclined one may be for Sunday travelling, necessity for it arises occasionally."[13] Some railway companies opposed Sunday services on humanitarian grounds, as their operation could involve staff in seven-day working.

So how did train service provision in London change during the period under review? Clearly the opening of new lines brought increased services, but on many routes existing in 1871 the changes up to 1900 were modest. Two articles published in the *Railway Magazine* in 1907 compared local train services in and around London at that time with what had existed in 1872 – a close approximation to the time period now under consideration. The author presents a mass of detail based on painstaking examination of the timetables. Some of his conclusions are surprising.

On the SER line to Addiscombe Road (Croydon) via Catford, for example, there were very few additional trains in 1907 compared with 1872. On the LCDR Metropolitan Extension (Loughborough Junction to Ludgate Hill), the 1872 train service was already "a very full one, and corresponded closely to that of today in general features. Many of the trains can be traced almost unaltered in the present timetables, a rather remarkable feature". On the LSWR the pattern of local service had not greatly changed, although there were more trains than in 1872.

North of the river, the author found more striking differences. On the GNR, the opening of new branches had substantially increased the number of trains since 1872: "The Great Northern Railway's local timetable was a very different compilation in those days... there being none of the complications which now render [it] so difficult to follow". But the most

10.   *SLP* 2.7.1898
11.   Sekon p. 196
12.   *North Metropolitan & Holloway Press* 16.9.1876; Jackson A/Borley H, *The Memories and Writings of a London Railwayman* (1993) p. 53
13.   *HFPJ* 3.7.1897

remarkable increases of all had occurred on the GER, whose 1872 timetable had changed out of all recognition by 1907.[14]

Who Used the Trains?

It has been estimated that, in 1875, between 150 million and 170 million journeys were made on London's local rail services – that is 36–40 journeys per head of population.[15] By 1901 this had risen to about 300 million journeys, or 45 journeys per head, though some sources give usage figures appreciably lower or higher than this.[16] The differences probably arise from varying definitions of "local rail services". But it seems likely that journeys roughly doubled over this period, while population increased by just under sixty per cent. Of the daily weekday arrivals in central London on suburban trains in 1901, just over sixty per cent were travelling to work.

A relatively small proportion of London's resident suburban population travelled by train to work in central London in the late nineteenth century. One south London study of 1890 suggested that no more than twenty-five per cent of the working population travelled daily to central London by all forms of public transport. In the north-east London suburbs served by the GER, however, with the benefit of cheap workmen's trains, this figure rose to around fifty per cent.[17] As one writer has observed, "the proportion of non-commuting residents in middle-class suburbs was far higher than in working-class ones, for the middle-class family demanded more people – both as household servants and in the local service industries – to provide for their needs and comforts".[18]

Passenger usage figures from individual railway company reports give little indication of local rail travel in London, except for the few companies whose operations were wholly within the London area – the Met, MDR, NLR and East London Railway. In 1875, between sixty and seventy per cent of local journeys were made on the services of these "metropolitan" companies.[19] User figures for individual stations are hard to come by, and those quoted for most London termini do of course include longer distance traffic. However, it is worth noting that a City of London one-day census in 1891 recorded roundly 52,000 passengers arriving at Liverpool Street, 43,000 at Broad Street, and 13,000 at Bishopsgate Street (Met), the last two being almost wholly local to London. The only other London terminus with more passengers than Broad Street was Victoria.[20]

Translating annual local journeys into daily figures and applying them to the number of stations served, it appears that towards the end of the nineteenth century an average London suburban station would have been handling about 1,000 to 1,500 originating journeys per weekday. There were of course wide variations around this mean: the outer ends of suburban

14.   *Railway Magazine* Nov/Dec.1907
15.   Barker & Robbins p. 165
16.   Kellett p. 92, White p. 96; Kellett implies 243 million, White gives 357 million.
17.   Kellett pp. 369, 376
18.   Olsen D, *The Growth of Victorian London* (1976) p. 310
19.   Barker & Robbins p. 165; services over the East London Railway were provided by the LBSCR at this time.
20.   *ROG* Aug.1891; *North London Railway: A Pictorial Record* (1979) pp. viii–ix

branch lines would doubtless have generated fewer passengers per station, while some inner suburban stations attracted many more. At Earlsfield (LSWR), for example, a well-used inner suburban station for which some data are available, there were about 6,000 daily weekday originating journeys in 1892.[21]

Weekday user figures can appear modest, however, when compared with weekend, Bank Holiday and excursion traffic to some of the principal leisure attractions. On Whit Monday 1873, the first Bank Holiday after the opening of the Alexandra Palace, 60,000 visitors travelled to the palace and its grounds, mostly on GNR trains. This exceeded the number visiting the rival Crystal Palace on that day. When the Alexandra Palace reopened in 1875 after the fire, Whit Monday saw no fewer than 94,000 visitors. Even when the palace itself was temporarily closed, substantial numbers travelled by train on Bank Holidays just to visit the park; on August Bank Holiday in 1884 about 35,000 arrived by GNR and GER trains. With the palace open again in 1898, 100,000 visited on Easter Monday.[22] This exceeded the total weekday usage of the whole GNR suburban system.

The strains placed on an individual station and its staff by the pressure of Bank Holiday traffic are illustrated in a report on the activity at Richmond Station on Easter Monday 1899. So popular was the destination that as many as thirty-seven special trains terminated there, and the same number returned, the traffic being shared by the LSWR, NLR and MDR. This was in addition to a similar number of specials calling on their way to and from other destinations, and to a modified local service. Over 15,000 tickets were issued at the station, and over 22,000 were collected. The writer of the report had some sympathy with the hardworking station staff, who were "robbed of all enjoyment" when the holiday traffic was in full swing.[23]

ALEXANDRA PALACE

VIEW FROM MUSWELL HILL

OPEN WET OR FINE
ORDINARY ADMISSION 1/- or by GUINEA SEASON TICKET

21. *Putney & Wandsworth Borough News* 25.6.1892
22. Davies R, *Rails to the People's Palace* (1980) pp. 10–11; Young p. 62; *HFPJ* 6.6.1884, 8.8.1884
23. *RTT* 8.4.1899

CHAPTER 3

INFORMATION AND FARES

A Choice of Maps

Without a map, planning all but the simplest journeys on London's late Victorian railway system would have been a daunting task. A range of maps was available to the intending traveller, but some needed to be used with caution as it was not unknown for even the most reliable publishers to include lines not yet built, or in some cases lines that never were built.[1]

Many railway maps of the period were produced by commercial publishers on their own account, rather than on behalf of railway companies. Among the most accurate, though available in limited numbers, were those published by John Airey, an employee of the Railway Clearing House. Airey's *Railway Map of London and its Suburbs* for 1870 was reproduced on a scale of two inches to the mile. It extended north to Crouch End, east to Charlton, south to Streatham, and west to Brentford. It showed distances between railway stations, and gave information on running powers and working arrangements between railway companies. In 1895 Airey sold his business to the Railway Clearing House, which continued to publish his map in broadly the same form up to the end of the century and beyond.[2]

Charles Dickens (junior) had this to say about Airey's map in his *Dictionary of London* (1888):

> It is almost unique in its way, devoting itself to its subject with a singleness
> of purpose which is really almost sublime, and absolutely ignoring all such
> minor features of the country it portrays as hills, roads, streets, churches,
> public buildings and so forth. ...It is only by such means that Mr. Airey attains,
> or can attain, his object, which is just to convey in simple but unmistakable
> form a considerable amount of curious information as to the ownership of
> the various lines which honeycomb the metropolis in every direction.[3]

Another important map publisher of the period was George Bacon, whose railway maps of London appeared either individually or as part of an atlas. Bacon's *Railway Guide*

---

1.   Hyde p. 16
2.   Hyde pp. 18–19, 131–134
3.   Dickens p. 156

Map of London and Suburbs for 1870 extended from Alexandra Park to Crystal Palace and from Richmond to Greenwich. Maps of similar extent, on a scale of one inch to the mile, continued to be published by Bacon up to the end of the century. Dickens was impressed with Bacon's map, judging it "near perfect", though the outline of principal streets was evidently not as up to date as the railway lines superimposed on them.[4]

Bradshaw's *Railway Station and Guide Map to the Environs of London* was perhaps rather too extended for convenient use within London, covering a radius of twenty-five miles from the centre on a scale of one third of an inch to a mile.[5] W.H. Smith's *Railway Station Map of London and its Environs* was more contained, extending from Edgware to Epsom and from Windsor to Chislehurst. Although this was sold as a general-purpose map, the heavily marked railway lines and stations showed up clearly above other features.[6] Both these maps were current during the 1880s.

Finally, among the commercial publishers, mention should be made of Newnes's *Royal Atlas of England and Wales*, 1899, which included as one of its many plates a railway map of London on a scale of one inch to a mile, extending from Highgate to Streatham and from Ealing to Woolwich. Although it was not made available separately from the atlas, it was a very clear piece of cartography, superimposing the railways on a topographical and relief map of London.[7]

Few railway companies sponsored the publication of London-wide maps in the late Victorian period. One exception was the MR, whose *London Railways Simplified and Explained* was published on the company's behalf by Charles Smith and Son. The railway lines, superimposed on street outlines, were distinguished by colour according to ownership, and where one company had running powers or working arrangements with another, the operating company's route was continued in the same colour alongside the "host" company's line. Further distinction between companies was achieved by the use of broken lines. In some cases as many as six lines, distinguished by colour and either broken or continuous, were shown running side by side over sections of line in multiple use. The result, said Dickens, was that:

> ...*the uninitiated student is astonished to find the Midland, the North-Western, and so forth, stretching out their feelers half way between London and Brighton, whilst on the other hand the London and Brighton line burrows under the river on its way to Liverpool Street, and the ubiquitous London, Chatham, and Dover thinks nothing of thrusting out its tentacles to Palmer's Green or Colney Hatch.*

This map was available through much of the period under review.[8]

---

4.   Hyde p. 175, Dickens p. 156
5.   Hyde p. 171
6.   Dickens p. 156
7.   Hyde p. 221
8.   Hyde p. 19, Dickens p. 156

Railway companies did publish system maps in their timebooks, sometimes as a fold-out or appendix, and these might include an enlargement for the London area. Not surprisingly, however, the companies gave prominence to their own routes and services, sometimes to the exclusion of other companies' lines. An example is the LNWR's London map, reproduced here from the company's April 1882 timebook. This shows in bold lines routes over which the LNWR operated, or which had advertised connections with LNWR services. Some other routes are shown as thin lines with few stations marked, and others, such as the MR from St. Pancras, are ignored altogether. The southern part of the Inner Circle, between Gloucester Road and Mansion House, is included because it carried the LNWR's Outer Circle service, but the remainder of the Inner Circle might never have existed! Clearly such a map would be of little use to anyone requiring a comprehensive guide to the London railway system.

The most highly regarded London railway map of the late nineteenth century was published by W.J. Adams for the MDR and known initially as the *District Railway Map of London*. It appeared in the 1870s on a scale of three and three quarter inches to the mile, and showed all the railways within an area bounded by Kentish Town, Brixton, Turnham Green and Stepney. Given that, at the time, the MDR did not extend far beyond central London, this rather limited compass was sufficient to show all the lines over which that company operated. The lines were superimposed on a street outline and topographical features.

In 1879 a new version appeared as the *Improved District Railway Map of London*. In order to embrace recent MDR extensions the scale was slightly reduced and the coverage increased to include Hampstead, Clapham and Ealing. Lines over which the MDR operated were shown in red, the "Inner Circle Completion Line" (the extension east of Moorgate Street) in blue, and other railways in black. The map was available in a linen wrapper at sixpence, mounted on linen at one shilling and sixpence, in a leather case at three shillings, and mounted on rollers and varnished at three shillings and sixpence. It received an enthusiastic welcome from the editor of the *Railway Sheet and Official Gazette*, not least for its clear depiction of topographical features and their relationship with the railway system:

> It supplies a want which has been long felt, and we predict for it the success that such an enterprise deserves. ...It might usefully be framed, glazed, and hung in every counting house in London.

The writer was clearly impressed with the amount of information on the back of the map. This included an order of stations, with their connections, on the Inner, Middle and Outer Circles, times of trains on the Met and MDR, and even particulars of "the various lights exhibited on the fronts of the engines, &c., so that the destination of each train may be readily known". Dickens too was high in his praise for this map, calling it "the best and most practically useful of all", and "absolutely indispensable". By 1900

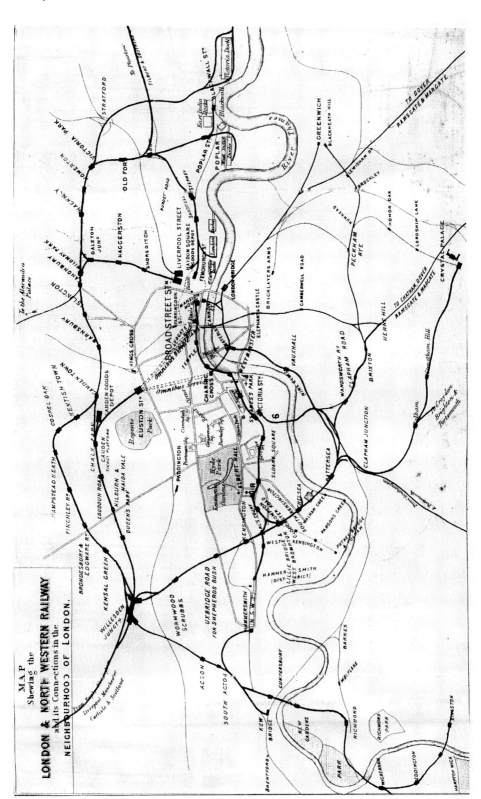

MAP
Shewing the
LONDON & NORTH WESTERN RAILWAY
and its Connections in the
NEIGHBOURHOOD OF LONDON.

From the LNWR timebook, April 1882

the *Improved District Railway Map* had run through six editions, with slight changes to the boundary and to line colouring. Its publication continued into the early years of the twentieth century.

In a further imaginative move, the MDR issued a "miniature" version of its map, on a scale of one inch to a mile, to publishers of London guide books, including those to the South Kensington exhibitions of the 1880s. By doing so the MDR not only saved the guide publishers the trouble of producing their own maps, but also received widespread publicity for its services at limited cost.[9] The railway map was no longer just a source of information; it was becoming a valuable advertisement for the rail services it portrayed.

What's in a Name?

Maps that related railway lines and stations to topographical features were particularly useful, not least because the names of some stations gave an imperfect indication of the localities they served.

Such was the case with stations named after long thoroughfares. Where, for example, in the whole length of Edgware Road, would the unprepared traveller expect to find the station of that name? In 1870 there were in fact two Edgware Road stations, more than two miles apart – one on the Met at Marylebone, the other on the LNWR at Brondesbury. The LNWR station later had "Brondesbury" added to its name. Finchley Road had no fewer than three stations bearing its name, on the LNWR, MR and Met, but in this case they were almost adjacent to one another. In 1880 the writer and local historian Edward Walford, a Hampstead resident, drew attention in the *Times* to the inconvenience caused by this.[10] The name "Frognal", which he suggested for the LNWR station, was shortly afterwards added to its name.

The earliest station in a locality would often take the historic parish or district name of the nearest settlement, even if the station were not centrally placed to serve it. When a new line was built to serve the locality more directly, new names had to be found for the stations upon it. These tended to be more localised and less widely known neighbourhood names, or even the names of thoroughfares. The original Tottenham Station of 1840, for example, was at the Hale, to the east of the historic settlement. When a new line, opened in 1872, served Tottenham more centrally, none of the new stations carried the name "Tottenham". Two years later a local resident expressed his dismay at the omission:

> *I have wondered what could have induced the Directors of the Line to*
> *name the stations so oddly as they have. "Seven Sisters" is not a place – I*
> *question whether a single resident in the parish adopts such an address;*
> *but West Green is. And who knows anything about Bruce Grove? Where*

9.   Hyde pp. 19–21, 149, 165–168, 171; Dickens p. 157; *RSOG* May 1879
10.   *Hampstead & Highgate Express* 18.9.1880; Edward Walford was co-author of *Old and New London* (1872–78) and author of *Greater London* (1883–84).

is it? – What is it? And White Hart Lane too. Either of these two might
conveniently have had the word Tottenham attached to them – the former
as Tottenham Road, or the latter as Lower Tottenham. I hope to see this
last-named title adopted even yet, as a substitute for the meaningless
White Hart Lane.[11]

The new names were retained, however, the GER no doubt wishing to avoid confusion with the existing Tottenham Station. As for Seven Sisters, a separate station called West Green would within four years be opened on the Palace Gates branch.

A similar but more complex example occurred in the Chiswick and Acton areas. "Stations bearing the names of 'Chiswick' and 'Acton' ", observed an 1886 editorial, "to which uninitiated visitors naturally come, are very inconveniently situated, so far as the most important centres of population and business are concerned". The writer pointed out that Chiswick Station (LSWR) was at Grove Park, about a mile to the south of Chiswick High Road, and Acton Station (GWR) was more than a mile north of the Acton High Road. Yet other stations, deriving their names from more local neighbourhoods, could, it was suggested, be called by the old parish names – Mill Hill Park becoming "Acton" and Turnham Green "Chiswick High Road". The writer believed that the name "Turnham Green" would fall out of use altogether "as the Vicar of Christ Church, Turnham Green, now publicly styles himself Vicar of Gunnersbury".[12]

Requests for station renaming also arose from residential development and population growth in expanding neighbourhoods, though these sometimes had as much to do with the potential for letting or selling new properties as with the convenience to the travelling public of a new station name. During the 1880s this became an issue in Finchley, on the High Barnet branch of the GNR. The station originally known as Torrington Park served the growing community of North Finchley, and the GNR was asked to adopt that name instead. The company refused, fearing confusion with Finchley (Church End) and East End (Finchley). But the agitation continued, and in 1882 a compromise was reached when the name was changed to Woodside Park for North Finchley. Four years later, users of East End (Finchley), disliking the class connotations of "East End", asked for a change to East Finchley, and this was agreed.[13] No doubt in this case the GNR recognised the revenue earning potential of a name devoid of working class associations.

Similar considerations inspired a 300-signature petition to the GNR in 1882 for the use of the name New Southgate in preference to Colney Hatch. Although both names were in use, Colney Hatch took precedence and was frequently called out by porters. Colney Hatch had become widely known as the name of the adjoining county lunatic asylum, and local residents disliked the connection:

---

11.   *Tottenham & Edmonton Weekly Herald* 24.10.1874
12.   *West London Observer* 4.12.1886; Mill Hill Park became Acton Town in the 20th century, but
       the name of Turnham Green remained unchanged.
13.   Wilmot G, *The Railway in Finchley* (1973) p. 29

*A large number of passengers who come down to see houses return
as soon as they find the station so designated in conjunction with New
Southgate... consequently only half of the houses are inhabited, which, if
occupied, would make a large and important town, and greatly increase
the revenue of your company.*

The petitioners also requested parcels to be labelled simply to New Southgate, "as
parties at a distance, unacquainted with the name of New Southgate, but knowing by repute
Colney Hatch, are unfavourably prejudiced against such an address". The petitioners were
successful; mindful no doubt of the revenue implications, the GNR agreed that the station
should be known simply as New Southgate, the words "For Colney Hatch" to appear in
smaller characters underneath on the station name boards.[14]

Timebooks

Bradshaw, the national railway timetable for the United Kingdom for well over a century,
needs little introduction. It began life in 1839 as *Bradshaw's Railway Companion*, being
replaced by *Bradshaw's Railway Guide* in 1842. By 1900 it contained well over a thousand
pages, giving the timetables of 160 railway companies. The price remained at sixpence from
1842 until 1915.[15] The book became a national institution, and no business, library or public
organisation of any kind could afford to be without it.

Dr. Watson was asked to consult *Bradshaw* when planning journeys for Sherlock
Holmes, but whether less educated folk would have been able to use the guide with similar
ease is open to question. For the Londoner wishing to plan local journeys in and around the
capital in the late nineteenth century, much thumbing and flicking of pages would have been
necessary, as the timetables were arranged by company, with local service and long distance
tables intermingled. For simple journeys to and from London termini, the *ABC Alphabetical
Rail Guide* would have been easier to use.

Alternatively, users may have turned to *Cassell's Time Tables*, first published in the
early 1860s. These, said the *Morning Post*,

*...may be safely recommended to all intent upon a railway journey, as
the clearly tabulated routes and the useful maps of the suburban and
provincial railway systems which they contain will enable the passenger
to select the train required without the slightest difficulty or uncertainty.*

From July 1886 these timetables were improved with the introduction of new type, an
entirely new railway map, and a clear distinction between day and night trains.[16]

---

14.   *North Middlesex Chronicle* 20.1.1883
15.   *Railway Magazine* May 1961
16.   Quoted in *West London Observer* 10.7.1886

As well as displaying sheet timetables at their stations, railway companies published their own timebooks, typically sold for one penny, and sometimes reissued monthly. They were available at stations, town offices and station bookstalls. More than one timebook would normally be needed for journeys involving interchange between the services of different companies, though some companies included details of connecting train services provided by other operators. In the early 1870s, for example, the MDR timetable contained "a great deal of information relating to other companies". The August 1872 issue extended to 144 pages, and was "almost becoming as formidable as 'Bradshaw' ".[17]

By the early 1880s the LNWR timebook was showing a wide range of connections with its Outer Circle and West London Line services at Dalston Junction, Willesden Junction and Kensington Addison Road, including trains to and from Blackwall (NLR), Alexandra Palace (GNR), Crystal Palace and Croydon (LBSCR) and Kingston (LSWR). It also showed connections between north-west England and the south coast by LNWR trains to and from Willesden, Kensington, Waterloo and Victoria. In common with other timebooks of the period, its layout and presentation would have made the reading of some tables difficult, not least because there was no variation in typeface to indicate which timings were for through trains and which necessitated a change of trains.

Boot and Son of Old Bailey published *Murray's London Time Tables* and the companion *Suburban Railway Guide*:

> *These useful little books, which can be carried in the waistcoat pocket, contain within a small space a vast amount of information, including complete timetables for all the metropolitan railways within 20 miles of London, a diary, complete list of cab and railway fares, and a map, showing the position of the various stations. One of these handbooks, ready for reference, would often save a great deal of trouble and inconvenience.*[18]

These were possibly the only really compact guides to the whole of London's late Victorian railway system.

More localised guides and timetables were produced from time to time, some of them short-lived. In 1890, for example, the *Kilburn Times* published details of a free "Railway, Omnibus and Tramway Guide" issued monthly by Macpherson's, a local coal merchant. Referred to as a "pocket diary and timetable", this gave information on public transport in Kilburn, Hampstead and Willesden, "and other information in a compact arrangement". "We understand", said the paper, "that a large edition has been 'snapped up' by the public".[19]

---

17.   *SLP* 3.8.1872
18.   *North Middlesex Chronicle* 16.6.1883
19.   *Kilburn Times* 17.1.1890

UP TRAINS CONTINUED—WEEK DAYS

Stations.		
CROYDON — dep.		
Second Junction		
CRYSTAL PAL. — dep.		
Gipsy Hill		
Lower Norwood		
Knight's Hill		
Balham		
Wandsworth Common		
Clapham Junction — arr.		
KENSINGTON — { dep. / arr. }		
WATERLOO — dep.		
Vauxhall		
Queen's Road		
MILNE HILL		
Britton and South Stockwell		
Clapham and North Stockwell		
Wandsworth Road		
VICTORIA (Brighton Railway)		
Battersea		
West Brompton (Lillie Bridge)		
KENSINGTON — arr.		
MANSION HOUSE — dep.		
Blackfriars (See Note A)		
Temple		
Westminster Bridge		
St. James's Park		
Sloane Square		
Brompton (Gloucester Road)		
Earl's Court		
VICTORIA (District Railway)		
KENSINGTON (Addison Road)		
Uxbridge Road (for Shepherd's Bush)		
WILLESDEN JUNCTION — { dep. / arr. }		
EUSTON — dep.		
Willesden		
Queen's Park		
Kilburn and Maida Vale		
Loudoun Road (for Swiss Cottage)		
Chalk Farm		
Willesden Junction — dep.		
Kensal Green		
Brondesbury		
Finchley Road and Frognal		
Hampstead Heath (Highgate)		
Gospel Oak		
Kentish Town		
Camden Town		
DALSTON JUNCTION — arr.		
Dalston Junc. dep. for Wood Green & Alex. P.		
Wood Green (for Alexandra Park)		
Alexandra Palace — arr.		
Dalston Junction — dep.		
Hackney		
Homerton		
Victoria Park		
Old Ford		
Poplar (East India Road)		
BLACKWALL — dep.		
Haggerston		
Shoreditch		
BROAD STREET — arr.		

Notes:

All London and North Western Trains convey 3rd Class Passengers between Mansion House, Willesden Junction, Kentish Town, and the Intermediate Stations.

Passengers for Barnsbury, Canonbury, Haggerston, and Shoreditch, change at Camden Town; and those for Hackney, Homerton, Victoria Park, Old Ford, Poplar, and Blackwall, change at Dalston Junction.

1—Passengers for Wood Green must change carriages at Finsbury Park on Saturdays only.

†—Steam car plys at frequent intervals between Blackfriars and London Bridge.

E—Dalston to Alexandra Palace on Wednesdays and Saturdays only.

I—Mondays and Thursdays only.

H—Trains marked H run to Willesden, High Level.

L—Trains marked L run to Willesden, Low Level.

P—The Trains marked P are Parliamentary Trains. All others are First, Second, and Third Class.

T—The Trains marked T are Through Trains as follows:—
Willesden to and from Victoria.
Willesden to and from Waterloo.
Willesden to and from Croydon.
Where the Trains are not so marked Passengers have to change carriages at Kensington.

Ordinary Tickets from Broad Street and North London Stations will be available if to or from London Road, or that Station, Finchley Road, or Hampstead Heath; if to or from Kilburn and Maida Vale, at that Station or Edgware Road; and if to or from Queen's Park, at that Station or Kensal Green.

Passengers holding Tickets from and to Kilburn and Edgware Road, Kensal Green and Queen's Park, Brondesbury and Kilburn, and Finchley Road and London, may use either Station on the L. N. W. Railway or the City, and all Stations on the North London Line, from Stations on the L. N. W. Railway north of Willesden, the North and South West Junction Railway, and the Richmond Extension Stations.

Extract from the LNWR timebook, April 1882, showing the Outer Circle service and its connections.

Fares – Fair or Unfair?

Rail fares could account for a substantial proportion of a regular traveller's income, and increases were greeted with disfavour by passengers who had become used to relatively stable fare levels. In 1873 the GNR announced a five per cent increase in the price of all its season tickets, prompting a call to the directors to examine their collective conscience:

> *If they have any of that article to spare, it ought to remind them that in arbitrarily raising their fares... they are inflicting a gross injustice upon persons who have permanently settled in the northern parts of Islington, Hornsey, and similar suburban neighbourhoods on the faith of calculations based upon the scale of charges made for travelling to or from business.* [20]

Similar indignation was expressed in 1877 by East Dulwich residents at the decision of the LBSCR to raise some fares by as much as twenty per cent. At a public meeting in January 1877 it was contended "that the reasonable fares hitherto prevailing had beguiled people into coming down there to live", and that first class passengers should respond by purchasing third class tickets, as "the only way to touch [the company] was through the pocket". Joint action was recommended with users of the LCDR, which had raised its fares at the beginning of January "without any previous notice". Some season ticket rates on the LCDR had risen by as much as thirty per cent. Increased fares between Walworth Road and Ludgate Hill, it was pointed out, "will chiefly fall on the working classes".[21]

People on low incomes were certainly sensitive to fares changes, even when these were relatively small. In the early 1880s the LCDR reduced the third class single fare from Elephant and Castle to Ludgate Hill from twopence to a penny; this caused "an enormous increase" in the number of passengers using Elephant. Then in 1883 the company increased the fare to three halfpence, with the result that "thousands of people" travelled instead by tramcar or on foot. A similar effect was felt at Camberwell New Road when the fare went up from twopence halfpenny to threepence. "In most instances the advance is felt very keenly by poor people journeying to and from their employment." [22]

---

20. *IG* 5.9.1873
21. *Camberwell News* 20.1.1877, 27.1.1877
22. *SLP* 6.10.1883

For leisure journeys too, railway fares could place a strain on the working man's pocket. In 1883 the GNR was urged to reduce fares for journeys to Alexandra Palace when it reopened to the public after a period of closure:

> *The fare to the Palace has always been one of the greatest hindrances to its success. If Paterfamilias and his wife and a couple of children went there, the railway alone often spoilt half-a-crown or three shillings before admission was gained. The outing, then, to the ordinary working man became not a very cheap one, for with three or four more shillings for admission and a little refreshment half-a-sovereign was gone, and not much seen for it. Now, in this age of enterprise, it is simply wonderful that railway companies have not discovered how, with a very cheap return fare, a great revenue might have been derived from passengers to the Palace and grounds at Muswell Hill.[23]*

Far from reducing fares for journeys to leisure attractions, railway companies were inclined to exploit the strength of their position as mass carriers and price upwards for such journeys. In May 1872 the MDR timed a fares increase to coincide with the first "shilling day" at the International Exhibition at South Kensington. "The act was not gracious: it may be doubted whether it was politic. Certainly it has awakened no little public indignation." The writer urged first and second class passengers to buy tickets for a lower class of carriage, thereby depriving the railway company of revenue.[24]

Public indignation was also directed at the LBSCR and LCDR in 1881 for setting fares to the Crystal Palace stations at an appreciably higher level than to the surrounding stations, and for increasing them still further on Bank Holidays. "The railway fares to the Palace are absurdly high", complained a journalist, making the palace "inaccessible save to those with money in their purses. ...Why should there not be a special price for visitors only?"[25]

In the absence of any standardised fares policy across the network, it was inevitable that pricing anomalies would occur, and some astute passengers were ready to exploit them. A passenger on the LSWR from Waterloo to Wimbledon discovered in 1881 that the return fare of one shilling and twopence could be reduced to elevenpence by changing and rebooking at Clapham Junction – "a pretty high premium on expedition".[26]

---

23. *North Middlesex Chronicle* 6.10.1883; Alexandra Palace was closed from Aug.1882 to March 1885.
24. *SLP* 11.5.1872
25. *SLP* 19.2.1881, 5.3.1881
26. *SLP* 7.5.1881

GREAT NORTHERN RAILWAY.

KEMPTON PARK RACES.

JUBILEE STAKES, May 12th.

RE-OPENING OF ALEXANDRA PALACE

SATURDAY, MAY 12th.

CRYSTAL PALACE. | ALBERT PALACE.

SATURDAY, May 12th, 1888,

CHEAP DAY EXCURSIONS TO

LONDON

and CRYSTAL PALACE, including admission,

WILL RUN AS UNDER :—

STATIONS.				TIMES.		Fares to KING'S CROSS & back.			
						First.		Third.	
				A.M.	A.M.	s.	d.	s.	d.
DUNSTABLE (Church Street)	... dep.			8 24	...	6	0	3	0
LUTON (G.N.)	,,			8 38	...	5	0	2	6
New Mill End	,,			8 42	...				
Harpenden	,,			8 50	...	4	0	2	0
Wheathampstead	,,			8 55	...				
Ayot	,,			9 2	...				
Hertford	,,			...	9 30	4	4	2	2
Hertingfordbury	,,			...	9 35				
Cole Green	,,			...	9 39				
ST. ALBANS (G.N.) ...	,,			...	9 38	3	6	1	9
Smallford	,,			...	9 45				
HATFIELD	,,			9 15	9 54				
FINSBURY PARK ...	... arr.			9 38	10 19				
LONDON (King's Cross) ...	,,			9 45	10 25				

Tickets will be issued by this excursion to Crystal Palace and back, including admission, at fares 2s. 3d. first class, and 1s. 6d. third class, higher than King's Cross fares.

RETURNING

same day only from LONDON (King's Cross) at 7.0 p.m., 9.30 p.m. and **12.0 midnight,** and from FINSBURY PARK at 7.7 p.m., 9.37 p.m. and **12.5 midnight.**

Children under three years of age, free ; above three and under twelve, half-fares. Tickets not transferable. The Company will not be responsible for luggage.

Persons leaving excursion trains at intermediate stations forfeit their excursion tickets and are required to pay the full ordinary fares.

Tickets to CRYSTAL PALACE and back, including admission to Palace, will be available on day of issue only, by ordinary trains between King's Cross (York Road platform) or either of L. C. & D. Co.'s London stations, and Crystal Palace High Level station.

Tickets, bills, and all particulars can be obtained at the stations.

London, King's Cross
April, 1888.
309/3,000—25-4-88.   Waterlow & Sons Limited, Printers, London Wall, London.

HENRY OAKLEY, *General Manager.*

GNR handbill of 1888 advertising fares by excursion trains to King's Cross. Alexandra Palace had been closed since September 1885. The Albert Palace, an exhibition and entertainments centre at Battersea Park, was opened in 1885.

Lack of consistency in the fares charged per mile for different journeys also invited adverse comment. In 1884, a Crouch End resident, signing himself "one that was had", queried why passengers on the NLR from Finsbury Park to Mildmay Park should pay as much for the journey as passengers to Broad Street, more than twice as far. He discovered that a first class return for the six-minute journey on the GNR from Crouch End to Finsbury Park cost fourpence, whereas a similar ticket from Finsbury Park to Mildmay Park – also six minutes – cost tenpence. "I should think no other trading community but a railway company would dare adopt such a system of overcharge."[27]

In 1889 a reporter for the *Richmond and Twickenham Times* presented a detailed comparison between fares on the LSWR from Richmond to Waterloo and fares from other stations a similar distance from the terminus. This demonstrated that fares were not based strictly on distance, and in one or two cases there were wide disparities. "Why Richmond people should pay twice as much as residents at Barnes for a first class return ticket between their station and Waterloo is a matter which passes comprehension." Such discrepancies were not found with LSWR season ticket rates from different stations, but a comparison with GER season ticket rates over similar distances to Richmond to Waterloo, from Enfield, Chingford and Chadwell Heath, revealed a marked bias in favour of the GER stations. "It cannot be wondered that many London business and professional men prefer to live in other suburbs when they are charged so excessively for season tickets at Richmond."[28]

Cheap fares for workmen were a separate but important issue on London's late Victorian railways. The first statutory workmen's trains were run by the LCDR in 1865, but the GER's provision soon became more extensive with the introduction of twopenny return fares between Walthamstow, Enfield, Edmonton and London. Other railway companies followed with rather less enthusiasm, but by 1882 nearly 25,700 workmen's tickets were being issued daily.

The Cheap Trains Act of 1883 strengthened the requirement to run workmen's trains, and pressure grew for yet more generous provision, backed by the National Association for the Extension of Workmen's Trains. Agitation continued to the end of the century, by which time the overcrowding of GER workmen's trains in north-east London had become legendary.[29]

---

27. *HFPJ* 7.11.1884
28. *RTT* 31.8.1889
29. See Pam D, *A History of Enfield*, Vol.2, *A Victorian Suburb* (1992). For a study of workmen's fares in south London 1860–1914 see H.Dyos in *Journal of Transport History*, May 1953.

"Half third return to Brixton, please."

"Half! What's your age?"

"I'm thirteen at home; but I'm only nine and a half on railways."

A SPEEDY RETRIBUTION

Small Boy. "'Arf ticket ter Baker Street."

[Pays, and awaits delivery of ticket

Clerk. "It's a shameful thing, a kid like you smoking!"

Small Boy (indignantly). "Who are yer callin' a kid? I'm fourteen!"

Clerk. "Oh, are you? Then you pay full fare to Baker Street!"

JUDGING BY APPEARANCES

Undersized Youth. "Now then, first return, Surbiton, and look sharp! How much?"

Clerk. "Three shillings. Half-price under twelve!"

Workmen alight at Victoria from a heavily loaded LCDR train from Ludgate Hill in 1865.

Two City of London stations opened in 1865 – Ludgate Hill (LCDR) *above* on 1st June, Broad Street (LNWR/NLR) *below* on 1st November. Both became busy and important stations for London suburban traffic in the late Victorian period. Ludgate Hill, on the Metropolitan Extension Line of the LCDR, handled cross-London services provided by as many as five railway companies on a wide selection of routes. Broad Street accommodated heavily loaded NLR trains from the inner and outer suburbs of north London, as well as the LNWR Outer Circle trains from Mansion House, Kensington, Willesden and Hampstead.

FROM THE GENERAL TO THE PARTICULAR

Young Lady (who has never travelled by this line before).
"Do you go to Kew Gardens?"
Booking-Clerk. "Sometimes on a Sunday, miss, on a
summer's afternoon!"

THE H GRATUITOUS

Lady. "Can I book through from here to Oban?"
Well-educated Clerk (correcting her). "Holborn, you
mean. No; but you can book to Broad Street, and then
take a 'bus!"

CHAPTER 4

STATIONS IN GENERAL

Starting the Journey

First impressions count, and to the late Victorian rail traveller in London the conditions experienced at the departure station could make or break the reputation of the railway company. The importance attached to station quality by the passenger is clear from the volume of public comment on this aspect of rail travel.

This chapter will take an overall view of station quality, drawing on reports of users' experiences across the network. The next chapter will explore in more detail the conditions facing passengers at stations on two busy lines and at two important interchange stations.

Railway Servants

In an age when automation and long distance communications systems were still in their infancy, the late Victorian rail traveller relied heavily on station staff – chiefly booking clerks, porters and ticket collectors – for assistance and information. The behaviour and performance of the railway servants with whom the passenger came in contact were therefore crucial in influencing public attitudes to the railway companies.

For most passengers, the first point of contact was the booking clerk. At smaller stations there would probably be just one clerk on duty, and if trains were fairly infrequent he might open his window only when departure time was approaching. At larger stations there might be separate windows for first, second and third class bookings, and at junction stations or termini separate windows for different routes. At stations served by more than one railway company it was common practice to provide separate booking points. At Fenchurch Street, for example, separate windows were marked for LTSR, NLR, GER and London and Blackwall tickets.[1]

Regrettably, the behaviour of some booking clerks left much to be desired. An incident at Twickenham Station (LSWR) in 1870 provides an unwelcome example. The booking clerk, after issuing a ticket to a passenger, included in the change a French coin. This may have been a genuine mistake, but when the passenger objected the clerk lost his temper, accused the passenger of trying to steal money from the company, and called the police. The

---

1.   Course p. 267

passenger was arrested and held in custody overnight, but the case was dismissed by the magistrate, and the LSWR lost an action for false imprisonment and, no doubt, a large slice of its reputation. The outcome for the booking clerk is not recorded.[2]

In 1880 Edward Walford, the local historian whose concern over station naming has been noted already, complained of the lack of "common civility" shown by the Met booking clerks at Finchley Road and the MR booking clerks at Moorgate Street. He suggested that a petition of local residents should be sent to the railway company directors, as "remonstrances from individuals on such subjects are useless, as I have found by experience".[3]

Further accusations of incivility among booking clerks, and of their "snobbishness", surfaced in south London in 1892:

> *A booking clerk is a booking clerk, and no amount of churlishness will make him either stationmaster or chief inspector. Civility costs nothing, but if they are fully convinced that their duties are beneath them I would advise them to steer for home.*[4]

Sometimes it was the shortage of booking clerks that provoked anger. In 1894 a late night passenger from Euston, travelling only as far as Kilburn, had to wait patiently at the one booking window open "while a foreign sailor was making the booking clerk understand that he wanted to go to Glasgow by the night mail, which started half an hour after my train". The Kilburn passenger missed his train, prompting the uncharitable thought that "I never liked foreign sailors: I like them less now".[5]

Two years later John Burns, MP for Battersea, anxious to preserve the equanimity of his constituents who were also LBSCR passengers, observed that:

> *It would prevent loss of temper, time, and fares, and make for a sweeter temper to third-class passengers if the booking clerks at Victoria Station were increased in number, so that one clerk, occasionally two, were not compelled to try the impossible feat of issuing tickets at three windows besides attending to their books.*[6]

Once the passenger had purchased a ticket and arrived on the platform, the role of the porter assumed great importance. His task was not simply to carry luggage – indeed, at suburban stations this was often a minor part of his duties. He had to call out the destinations and stopping points of trains, announce the name of the station for passengers alighting, and answer enquiries. At interchange stations he would need to direct passengers to the correct platforms for onward connections. He also had a responsibility to ensure that passengers boarded and alighted from trains safely, and to deal with emergencies when they arose.

2.   *Illustrated London News* 12.2.1870
3.   *Hampstead & Highgate Express* 3.4.1880
4.   *BST* 6.8.1892
5.   *Kilburn Times* 23.11.1894
6.   *South Western Star* 28.2.1896

Not surprisingly, the effectiveness with which these tasks were performed varied considerably, and porters were often the target of criticism and occasionally abuse. At the same time there was widespread appreciation of how demanding their jobs could be, and some sympathy with them over the way they could be treated, as in this comment from south London in 1872:

> *Railway servants are sometimes gruff and far from obliging; but really they have a good deal to try their tempers. The stupid people who are always on the wrong platform, or will persist in getting into the wrong train, or make sure by asking the same question over and over again, are inexpressibly trying.*

Moreover, as the writer goes on to relate, it was not unknown for passengers to provoke porters deliberately by asking them absurd questions:

> *One could not help laughing with a jolly party returning from the Crystal Palace the other night, who indulged their fun at several stations. "Porter", cried the blandest of the party. "Yes, sir." "Will you do me the favour of informing me the name of this station?" "Certainly, sir"; and he gave it. "Thank you. And what is the population of this place?" The porter wouldn't "know nothink about that". "Indeed! Is there a Roman Catholic Church in it, and are the population as a rule favourable to, or opposed to, vaccination?" But by this time the train was moving on.[7]*

The inability of railway porters to pronounce station names correctly was a frequent cause of complaint, the issue being elevated to a *Daily Telegraph* leader in 1879:

> *Language seems to be given to the railway porter to enable him to conceal his topography. "Madagascar" does not in the least resemble "Clapham Junction", nor does "Kiel" sound like "Denmark Hill", nor "Pondicherry" like "Holloway", nor "Siam" like "South Kensington", nor "Nishni Novgorod" like "Finsbury Park"; yet all these sounds are indistinctly heard by the fanciful ear in a short railway journey out of the central districts, being even as one pronunciation to him who calleth, and likewise to him who essayeth to hear and to understand. At our bustling suburban stations the consequent difficulty is not slight, and, in the hurry of local traffic, travellers are sometimes misled.[8]*

---

7.   *SLP* 21.12.1872
8.   Quoted in *RTT* 4.10.1879

The inconvenience to travellers of not being able to identify the names of stations "lustily bawled" by porters was highlighted in the same year by an LSWR passenger from Teddington to Hammersmith, who recorded the following pronunciations on his journey – Twicknem, Margrits, Ritchmönd, Gardings, Gunnersbree, Turnhim Green, Shafbree Road and 'Amersmith.[9] Passengers familiar with the localities would perhaps have understood, but strangers who did not know what Kew was famous for could well have been baffled by Gardings.

Far more serious was the occasional disregard of passengers' safety by careless or even reckless porters. At Walworth Road Station (LCDR) in June 1877, porters were accused of "chaffing and joking" instead of attending to their duties when a 14-year-old girl narrowly escaped injury after jumping onto the track to retrieve a dropped ticket.[10] At Mortlake Station (LSWR) in April 1879, a porter "scared it across" the line on a boarded foot crossing in front of an approaching train, and a passenger who followed his example came within inches of being struck by the engine.[11]

Ten years after this latter incident, however, we find a journalist full of praise for the servants and officials of the LSWR – "about the most civil lot of men of any English line of which I have any experience". His concluding remark is nonetheless laced with more than a little sarcasm:

> *I have heard something about a rich old gentleman who asked a porter what time the next train went somewhere or other, and was so pleased at the polite way in which the man answered that he added a codicil to his will when he got home, leaving him a large fortune, and died the following week.*[12]

Occasionally station staff were called upon to perform tasks well beyond their normal duties. In January 1881 a gentleman of "inordinate bucolic proportions" wished to travel on the LCDR from Walworth Road to Ludgate Hill. When the train came in he attempted to enter a third class compartment. Seeing that he was too big for the doorway, a station inspector gave him a push from behind, whilst passengers in the compartment pulled, but "his proportion of stomach was so large that he could not be put in even sideways!" When the next train arrived, the double doors of the brakevan were opened, and the portly gentleman was safely deposited inside.[13] The incident calls to mind the story of a female passenger of advanced years and ample proportions who could only alight from a train backwards. Every time she began to get out a porter would rush up to her crying "hurry up, ma'am, train's going" and push her in again.[14]

To foster pride in their appearance, the LCDR issued its station staff with new uniforms in 1898. Embellished with gold braid and brass buttons, they had a distinctly maritime look,

9.   *RTT* 31.5.1879
10. *Camberwell News* 30.6.1877
11. *RTT* 12.4.1879
12. *RTT* 14.9.1889
13. *SLP* 5.2.1881
14. *Railway Magazine* May–June 1944

HELPFUL
ASSISTANCE
IN ANY
EMERGENCY

prompting one inebriated passenger, when asked for his ticket, to declare, "I'll be hanged if I give my ticket to the steward!" The incident drew a comment from the journalist reporting it that, in their smart new uniforms, the railway officials looked "more like officers of the Queen's navee than the steward of a Channel steamboat".[15]

It was customary for passengers to tip station staff, especially porters, if they undertook special favours, though the practice was discouraged by the railway companies, and at many stations notices were displayed to the effect that company servants were prohibited from accepting gratuities. In a case brought to court in 1883, a passenger on the Met tipped a porter at Aldersgate Street Station for agreeing to look after his luggage during a short absence; when he returned, one bag was missing, but he discovered that by tipping the porter he had negated any liability the company might have had for the loss.[16]

Regular passengers would often show their appreciation of porters and ticket collectors by giving them Christmas boxes. Railway staff who did not come in contact with the public, but who provided a valuable service to them, were less fortunate. In 1882 a plaintive letter from a Hackney signalman pleaded with passengers to give their Christmas boxes to stationmasters, so that the donations could be shared among all the staff under their control.[17]

Finding the Way

Without the assistance of helpful staff, finding the right train, particularly at busy interchange stations, could be difficult. Some stations had a reputation for confusion. Willesden Junction (LNWR) earned the nickname "Bewildering Junction" largely because, until 1885, Broad

15. *SLP* 4.6.1898
16. *SLP* 7.7.1883
17. *Hackney & Kingsland Gazette* 15.12.1882

Street trains left alternately from two high level platforms separated from each other by two staircases and a low level platform. Many a passenger, missing one Broad Street train, made the pilgrimage to the alternative platform only to see the next Broad Street train pulling out. Finding the exit at this station could also be a challenge; it was alleged that the station was haunted by the ghosts of passengers who had long since expired while looking for the way out.[18]

Similar jokes were told at the expense of Waterloo, a terminus that developed piecemeal from its opening in 1848. The original station was enlarged on the north side in 1860, and in 1878 a completely separate station was added to the south (the "new station" or "Cyprus"). There was also a single-track loop line carried across the concourse of the original station to join the SER at Waterloo Junction. Passengers for Vauxhall or Clapham Junction who had just missed a train from the loop line platform and were redirected "would arrive at the new station after half a day's journey, and reach the top end of the Cyprus platform thoroughly exhausted... only to perceive the train on the move". So back to the loop line platform they went...

> *Those gentlemen who are fond of trying experiments with dynamite might turn their attention to Waterloo Station. No jury... would convict them for effacing such an abortion from the railway map as the present station at Waterloo.*[19]

That was the situation in 1881. A further addition to the station on the north side was made in 1885. Complete rebuilding did not commence until 1902.

Another problem for London rail passengers in a hurry was how to find the right class of carriage. The NLR simplified the task by making up trains in standard formations and displaying signs on the platform showing where each class of carriage would stop.[20] Similar provision was made on the Inner Circle, where speed of boarding was particularly important. Other companies instructed porters to call out the positions of the carriages when a train had stopped, though on at least one occasion the persistence of a porter at Denmark Hill Station in shouting repeatedly "third class in front" to a completely empty platform was a source of some amusement to passengers in the train.[21]

Passengers who were unsure whether the train had arrived at their intended destination were not helped by the generally sparse provision of station name boards and their subordination to advertising, particularly on the Inner Circle. The names of stations were sometimes so lost among advertisements "that, looking from the carriage, you appear to have reached Caracca Cocoa, Ozokerine, or Antipelliculaire".[22] Indeed, trying to distinguish any source of information from the commercial clutter on platforms could have interesting

18.   Robbins p. 14; Sekon pp. 165–166
19.   *SLP* 28.5.1881; "Cyprus" was so called because it was opened in the year in which Britain acquired the island of that name.
20.   Robbins p. 24
21.   *SLP* 30.5.1874
22.   *SLP* 11.4.1874

results: "A few days ago", wrote a correspondent in 1886, "when impatiently waiting for a train, a faithful believer in railway time was seen to alter his watch by the dial on the weighing machine at Westbourne Park Station!"[23]

Cold Comfort

The inadequacies of waiting rooms and shelters at suburban stations were a major source of complaint. Exposure to the elements was not simply a matter of discomfort; ill health and even death were attributed to it. Hampstead Heath Station (LNWR) was described in 1880 as "a huge death-trap for the delicate, exposed as it is both to the blast of the east wind and to the draught coming from the tunnel", and it was alleged that more than one fatal attack of bronchitis had resulted from waiting there for trains.[24]

Three years later a correspondent from New Southgate penned what he called a "subdued growl" about the condition of the GNR station there. In summer, "when all love the open air", he could tolerate the miserable waiting rooms on the up platform, but not during the long "winter of our discontent". He invited one of the directors of the company to wait there for a down train on a cold, dreary December night, when he would "find to his astonishment that on the down platform there is not a single waiting-room, the only makeshift in the way of shelter being a shed open on three sides to the beating rain and the searching wind".[25]

Although public health provision began to improve during the late Victorian period, cities could still be hazardous places in which to live. It would be easy to dismiss with amusement the claim that a draughty railway station posed a threat to public health. But for the more vulnerable members of society, a quarter of an hour spent without protection on a freezing station platform, and more particularly in a thick London fog, could spell disaster for chest and lungs. This letter of February 1895 from a Peckham resident, who had clearly experienced the exposed, windswept platforms of the South London Line, reflected a real concern for his fellow travellers:

> *I take the opportunity of this Siberian weather to say what a comfort a*
> *small nook out of these severe and dangerous winds would be to delicate*
> *persons waiting for their trains at Queen's Road, Old Kent Road, and*
> *South Bermondsey Stations.*[26]

Even where adequate waiting rooms were provided, lack of heating within them could create a "winter of discontent". In the opening months of 1879, passengers hoping to warm themselves while waiting at Brentford Station (LSWR) could feel "not an ember", though there was an ample fire in the porters' room. "For the authorities to so often deprive their passengers of a little warmth from the tiniest of fireplaces during

23.   *ROG* Nov.1886
24.   *Hampstead & Highgate Express* 20.3.1880
25.   *North Middlesex Chronicle* 8.9.1883
26.   *South London Observer* 9.2.1895

this rather inclement season is what ought not to be."[27] In January 1881 passengers at Vauxhall Station (LSWR) endured a "tremendous snowstorm" with only "miserable fires" in the waiting rooms. A correspondent observed that some railway companies allowed stationmasters free coals for their own households, and wondered whether they would be as economical with the use of fuel in their own homes as in the uncomfortable waiting rooms at Vauxhall.[28]

Provision of public lavatories at stations was an important factor in encouraging mobility in the railway age; indeed, without them, ladies especially would not have been able to contemplate any but the shortest journeys. Although there was reticence among passengers to comment publicly on the condition of station lavatories, criticisms did surface from time to time, as at Turnham Green (LSWR) in February 1889:

> *The sanitary arrangements at some of the stations round London are simply disgusting. We may instance those connected with the ladies' waiting room (booking office side) at Bedford Park* [i.e. Turnham Green], *to which attention was called... some time ago. Many months have now elapsed, and still things are no better. There appears to be the same need of adequate ventilation, the same loathsomeness, and the same official indifference, with the consequent risk to health and offence to the public.*

We are spared a detailed account of the conditions, but the writer observes that "the nuisance is one that ladies feel some reluctance in complaining about", and their unwillingness to do so made it harder to get improvements carried out.[29]

Twinkles of Light

Many suburban stations were sparsely lit after dark throughout the late Victorian period. During the 1870s and 1880s they relied on fish-tail gas burners, and at smaller stations the lamps were turned up only when a train was calling.[30] This could be a cause of inconvenience to passengers obliged to wait on the station for lengthy periods. On one dark evening in February 1883, an LCDR passenger at Clapham Station on the South London Line, having just missed his train, had to wait half an hour for the next. But as soon as he sat down in the waiting room to read his newspaper, the gas was turned down so low that reading became impossible. On enquiring of a porter why only a "dim twinkle of gas" was permitted in the waiting room, the passenger was told that it was turned down on the company's orders as "too much gas had been used"![31]

---

27. *RTT* 1.3.1879
28. *SLP* 22.1.1881, 29.1.1881
29. *RTT* 2.2.1889
30. Sekon pp. 199–200
31. *SLP* 3.3.1883, 10.3.1883

Any failure of the gas supply plunged stations into darkness, and staff had to find what emergency lighting they could. In 1872 a strike of gasworks stokers interrupted the supply of gas to many London stations: naphtha lamps were brought in to light stations on the Met and MDR, while oil carriage-lamps were used at Ludgate Hill.[32]

Advertisers as well as passengers were dissatisfied with the poor quality of gas lighting at stations. In 1872 complaints were made that, although stations on the MDR were thickly studded with advertisements, it was almost impossible to see them by the "feeble glimmer" of gas supplied. "Now the sole object of those paying large sums for the privilege of exhibition is that of being seen."[33] Invention of the incandescent mantle in the late 1880s greatly improved the standard of gas lighting, but some smaller stations retained their fish-tail gas jets well into the 1890s.

Experiments with electric lighting began in the late 1870s. In December 1878 the LBSCR lit the space between the booking offices and platform barriers at London Bridge Station with an electric lamp that burned for twelve hours without attention.[34] A successful trial of electric lights at Liverpool Street during 1880 was extended from main-line to suburban platforms towards the end of that year. At the same time the MDR lit its Charing Cross Station with three electric lights on the exterior and seven on the platforms, which "sprang into a soft but brilliant radiance as if by magic, and very much to the surprise of some hundreds of passengers".[35] Electric lighting also reached Paddington main line station in 1880, and King's Cross and Waterloo in 1881.[36] By the early 1890s the installation at Paddington had become very large, leaving a deep impression on one contributor to the *English Illustrated Magazine*:

> *At night, standing under the bridge just where the steps come down from Bishop's Road Station and looking outwards, the scene is most impressive and weird. High in the air gleam two great electric lights, the apexes of two ghostly pyramids of light, around* [which] *swirls the steam of passing engines, beneath all is rush, swish, and darkness, and innumerable coloured lights twinkling and blurred. Everything seems in motion except the two gleaming eyes looking down with steady sphinx-like shine.*[37]

32. *Illustrated London News* 14.12.1872
33. *SLP* 5.10.1872
34. *East London Observer* 28.12.1878
35. *RSOG* Sept/Nov.1880
36. Course p. 251, *SLP* 12.2.1881
37. Reprinted in *Railway Magazine* July–Aug.1944

Buffets and Bars

Station refreshment rooms were a popular target for music-hall jokes. The steaming tea urns, curling sandwiches, stale pies and unhelpful staff were easily parodied. The scene would have been all too familiar to a journalist who entered the refreshment bar at Waterloo Station late one evening in 1889. He had to ask the barmaid five times for a pint of ale before it was served – and then it came in a dirty glass. Whilst conceding the barmaids "a great deal of sympathy with respect to the insults and annoyances they are continually subjected to from divers individuals of the male sex", he felt that a quiet and decently behaved person such as he should have been better treated. His experience was evidently not uncommon: "very likely one of these days... I shall let myself go on the subject, and then the refreshment contractors and their assistants will have to look out".[38]

Railway catering was not universally bad, however, and some of the establishments were of a high standard, especially where full restaurant service was provided. Outstanding in this respect was the Silver Grill at Ludgate Hill Station, opened by the railway catering pioneers Spiers and Pond in 1866. Situated in a "great, yawning railway arch", it earned the compliments of Charles Dickens in *All the Year Round*, while another writer appreciated the "neat, sprightly, well-dressed misses of the Ludgate Hill Bar". The place became a well-known rendezvous during the late Victorian period.[39]

More modest but widely welcomed was "a handsome refreshment buffet and commodious dining-room" opened in 1872 in a railway arch at Vauxhall Station. The proprietor was Mr. W.H. Clark "whose satisfactory catering at other stations is so well known and appreciated by travellers on the South-Western system". Anticipating a wealthy clientele from Belgravia and Pimlico, the proprietor had "engaged a staff of Hebes for the buffet, and attendants in the dining-room in fitting character with their gorgeously-appointed surroundings".[40]

The much maligned LCDR was, in regard to station catering, generous in its provision of well-appointed "light refreshment tea rooms and buffets" at inner London stations, including Herne Hill, Brixton and Loughborough Junction. Other companies provided refreshment rooms at their main line termini, whilst the Met and MDR had them at principal stations on the Inner Circle, including Baker Street, King's Cross, Sloane Square and Victoria.[41] The buffet at Farringdon Street Station was in fact the first London venture of Spiers and Pond, opened in 1863.

A Cursory Inspection

Railway management was often accused of ignoring passengers' complaints, or of simply being unaware of the local situation. The accusation was not always fair. Representations, often in the form of "memorials" or deputations, could lead to improvements, and directors would from time to time go out and see for themselves. However, if a reported account by an outside observer of a station inspection at Richmond in 1879 is to be believed, management may have returned with an alarmingly superficial knowledge of the problems passengers faced:

> *The train having stopped, the directors alighted, and were escorted through the various rooms on the down platform, this course taking but a few minutes; after which, they passed round the head of the train on to the up platform, spent a considerable part of the fifteen minutes that were allotted to them to examine this station in the refreshment bar, continued their walk through the platform, taking a cursory glance at the new station [terminal platforms], passed round the back of the train, took their seats, and went on with their journey.*

How could these gentlemen, asks the writer, "see through brick walls, look into the nooks and corners, and ferret out, as they are supposed to do, anything that may require to be done for the benefit of the travelling public?"[42] Presumably they did at least come away with a good understanding of the catering arrangements at Richmond Station!

SO LIKELY!

Scene—*Bar of a railway refreshment-room.*
Barmaid. "Tea, sir?"
Mr. Boozy. "Tea!!! ME!!!!"

BEHIND THE SCENES

Head Barmaid. "These tarts are quite stale, Miss Hunt—been on the counter for a fortnight! *Would* you mind taking them into the *second - class* refreshment-room?"

42. *RTT* 29.11.1879

CHAPTER 5
STATIONS IN PARTICULAR

Metropolitan Extension: Cheerless and Forlorn

The stations on the LCDR Metropolitan Extension Line from Loughborough Junction to Ludgate Hill were probably the subject of more comment and criticism in the late Victorian period than any other group of stations in London. Some of them were busy, but all were unloved. We will look in some detail at the experiences of users of five of these stations.

Loughborough Junction

Loughborough Road Station became Loughborough Junction in 1872 with the opening of a new curve to Denmark Hill on the South London Line and the introduction of a through service between Ludgate Hill and Crystal Palace. The story begins on an optimistic note with extensive rebuilding and enlargement of the station to accommodate the additional trains and passengers. Six new platforms were constructed to serve the three lines converging at the station; they were accessed by spacious corridors, galleries and staircases from the ground level booking offices and waiting rooms. The platforms were canopied for much of their length, and a large waiting room was provided on the Crystal Palace platform. With these improvements, Loughborough Junction was expected to become one of the busiest intermediate stations on the LCDR.[1]

Not long after its opening, however, the enlarged station began to attract criticism. Initially this concerned the approaches to it from Coldharbour Lane and Loughborough Road; the former involved wading through "a perfect quagmire", the latter required an uncomfortable walk across loose gravel which "the traffic and the wet weather will speedily convert into mud".[2] Passengers did appreciate "the uniform civility of the servants who do duty at the station", and especially "the gentleman with the stentorian voice who stands in the corridor to direct passengers up the various staircases". But the eccentricities of the platform porters' pronunciation were, as elsewhere, a source of amusement and irritation – Loffboro', Laffbro' and Larfboro' Juncshin being among the variants heard. More amusing

---

1. *SLP* 21.9.1872
2. *SLP* 14.12.1872

and irritating than this, however, were the races that occurred from platform to platform every morning as trains for the City, arriving at any one of the three up platforms, attracted "a general stampede" from the others. "On the whole there are places in the world duller than Loughborough Junction", concludes the writer.[3]

Twenty years after the enlarged station had been opened, a contributor to a local newspaper, signing himself "The Peripatetic Quill", penned an article about the community surrounding the station, the whole area having by that time become known as Loughborough Junction. His comments about bad paving, muddy roads, and the din of heavy carts rumbling and clattering over the multiplicity of tram lines could have applied to many London suburbs, but the numerous railway arches were, he claimed, "not merely the gloomiest, but the noisiest to be found in a day's march". And at the station itself, the strong-voiced porter, or his successor, was still yelling out his directions to passengers.[4]

Walworth Road

One of the least appreciated suburban stations on the LCDR must surely have been Walworth Road. Though thousands used the station daily, it lacked proper waiting rooms, let alone "retiring-rooms for ladies". The "dingy and neglected structure" was cleaned and decorated in 1872, but four years later it was still being referred to as a "chamber of horrors", where the traveller "will be able to see how a naturally ill-constructed building is ingeniously rendered still more inconvenient by bad arrangements and indifference to the comfort of the travelling public".[5]

At a public meeting at Peckham in July 1877 a further problem was highlighted: the LCDR had let some of the arches beneath the platforms to tenants who lit fires in them, causing the smoke to rise through the wooden boarded platforms and smother the waiting passengers. The meeting concluded that "the conduct of the company in converting the Walworth Road Station into a chimney shaft is deserving of great censure".[6] (A similar problem apparently arose later at Brixton Station, but in this case the culprit was a forge operated by the LCDR for the manufacture of signals and signal-posts.[7])

Relief for the users of Walworth Road was slow to arrive. In 1887 the station was described as a "ramshackle higgledy-piggledy arrangement of arches", and a female passenger wrote: "although suffering from a weak chest, I had to sit for over a quarter of an hour in an open shed looking at dirty surroundings, and inhaling the choking fog of a London November morning".[8] Matters came to a head in April 1889 with a public meeting of Walworth and Camberwell residents, chaired by the MP Mr. Radcliffe Cooke. The meeting received a petition with over 10,000 signatures protesting at the inadequacies

---

3.   *SLP* 5.9.1874
4.   *BST* 6.8.1892
5.   *SLP* 21.9.1872, *Camberwell News* 23.12.1876
6.   *Camberwell News* 28.7.1877
7.   *SLP* 15.6.1889
8.   *South London Chronicle* 26.11.1887

A BREEZY STATION.

COMING DOWN "THE SHOOT."

MAKING FOR "THE SHOOT."

of Walworth Road Station, which had become a "public scandal".

The four-track railway at Walworth Road was served by two side platforms and one central island platform. Access to the island platform was by a long, narrow and steeply sloping passage known locally as the "Walworth Shoot". Wholly inadequate for the large crowds using the station, this infamous feature became the target of cartoons and humorous comment over many years. Here is one example, following the public meeting in 1889:

> *So famous has this interesting platform-exit become, that people have been*
> *known to travel thousands of miles to see it. ...When "The Shoot" is in full*
> *working order – that is, when it is shooting itself of passengers, much after*
> *the ways of a coal sack – a very curious sight is witnessed. Men, women*

and children of all ages and sizes rub shoulders together... sorrowful in having to brave the perils, the squeezings, "scrimmagings", screamings, and swearings inevitably associated with "going down the shoot".

The meeting resolved that a deputation would present the petition to the directors of the LCDR.[9]

Six weeks passed before the deputation was received, but in response the LCDR did promise improvements at Walworth Road, including a better booking office and a ladies' room.[10] Some changes were made, but three years later, in 1892, a report by the Highways Committee of the London County Council found the alterations unsatisfactory, and recommended that further work be undertaken. This included abolition of the famous "shoot" and its replacement by a staircase.[11] Thus did a small curiosity of London's late Victorian railways pass into history.

Elephant and Castle

"It would almost seem as if the London, Chatham, and Dover Railway Company took a pride in rendering their stations as uncomfortable as possible", wrote a reporter in 1872, adding that "the Elephant and Castle may be selected as a representative of the others in point of dirt and want of accommodation". But the Elephant had its own particular nuisance in the form of a "detestable odour" assailing the nose of the waiting or alighting passenger. Our intrepid reporter investigated, and discovered that arches beneath the station were being used as stables by a cab proprietor. The manure was being allowed to accumulate until it was in a putrid state. And worse was to come. The same area was being used by a butcher to dress carcasses intended for human consumption. "I should certainly recommend an inspector of nuisances to visit the Elephant and Castle Station."[12]

Two years later the Elephant again attracted notice with the opening of a refreshment bar on the central island platform. This was greeted with surprisingly unfavourable press comment – to the effect that the money would have been better spent at other stations, notably on improving "the wretched collection of grimy sheds" at Walworth Road. The writer pointed out that Elephant and Castle Station was already surrounded by public houses; "one is tempted to ask whether this introduction is prompted by a desire on the part of the company to study the wants of the public or to benefit their own pockets".[13] Given the negative response to the LCDR's performance generally, it seems unfortunate that the provision of a new station refreshment room should have been so grudgingly received.

---

9. *SLP* 4.5.1889, *London Railway Record* April 2005
10. *SLP* 29.6.1889
11. *BST* 2.4.1892, 9.4.1892, 23.4.1892
12. *SLP* 17.2.1872
13. *SLP* 4.7.1874

Borough Road

And so to poor, neglected Borough Road, made even "more dismal" in 1881 by its pathetic attempt to celebrate Christmas:

> *Some melancholy porter, with nothing better to do, has gone to the trouble*
> *of decorating the posts which support the covering to the platform on the*
> *up side! The struggle of this unlucky station to appear "jolly" is enough*
> *to make one shed tears.*

Perhaps, said the writer, the decorations were meant as a satire, as he believed that no other stations on the Extension Line had exhibited similar signs of festive rejoicing.[14]

To one observer in 1889, the "much maligned" Borough Road was "sepulchral in character", exerting its baleful influence over all who used it:

> *People walking along the platform invariably remind one of a funeral*
> *procession. I never yet saw a Borough Road passenger laugh, smile,*
> *engage in conversation with a fellow passenger, talk to the station master,*
> *or crack a nut or a joke! The surroundings... exercise an enormous*
> *influence on the few people who use the station, and especially in the dark*
> *hours – and after sunset all the hours at the Borough Road are dark. ...*
> *But even in the daytime the whole place has a fearsome, a forbidding, a*
> *terribly chilling effect.*

The effect was heightened by "the very peculiar sub-platform arrangements" at Borough Road. The suffocating smoke at Walworth Road, and the noxious odours at the Elephant, were bad enough, but the offensive smell emanating from the subterranean regions of Borough Road was nothing less than that of decaying human remains. "There is nothing like it in the whole world of stationland. It is peculiar to the Borough Road – entirely *sui generis*." And yet:

> *I, for one, would not have the station removed, or renovated, or beautified.*
> *It serves the one grand purpose of making one more satisfied with other*
> *stations on the line, which, in comparison, stand out as light, cheerful,*
> *well-arranged specimens of station architecture.*[15]

Ludgate Hill

During the 1870s the LCDR's suburban traffic continued to grow, to the point where Ludgate Hill Station became "overtaxed and terribly congested". Pressure mounted for the

---

14.   *SLP* 31.12.1881
15.   *SLP* 25.5.1889

reconstruction of the station, which had become "neither more nor less than a disgrace".[16] But instead the company responded with other plans to increase the capacity of its City stations, initially with the opening of Holborn Viaduct Station in 1874, then with the widening of Blackfriars railway bridge and the opening of St. Paul's Station in 1886.

Helpful though these improvements were, they did not address the deteriorating condition of Ludgate Hill, described by Charles Dickens (junior) in 1888 as "dirty, ramshackle and altogether deplorable".[17] In the following year a newspaper columnist wrote at length about the station:

> *The booking-office at Ludgate is seen at its best about six or seven o'clock, when a "tail" as long as the sea serpent may be seen extending from the third-class Victoria and [Crystal] Palace peephole. It is smelt at its best about five o'clock, when the booking-clerks are cooking their herrings. Then the passengers get more than the ticket demanded.*

To reach the ladies' retiring room at the station, female passengers had to pass through the so-called "first-class waiting room":

16. *SLP* 12.2.1881, 25.6.1881
17. Dickens p. 116

> *A dark, dirty-looking, half-furnished, mysterious kind of hole in the wall.*
> *It is in a deplorable state of repair is this "first-class" room, and for*
> *elegance and comfort might compare unfavourably with the worst third-*
> *class waiting room yet born!*

A less threatening though even more mysterious feature of the station was a tall gentleman known as General Promenader. He could be seen circulating at all hours of the day and night, rarely speaking but always observing. Was he, asks our columnist, a gentleman from Scotland Yard, a prince in disguise, a railway census official, an actor out of collar, a peripatetic philosopher, a student of the fashions, a go-as-you-please professor of pedestrianism, or a censor of morals? The question is not answered. With or without General Promenader, however, Ludgate Hill Station was judged to be "unique for inconvenience, discomfort, and appearances. ...[It] is only like itself, and nothing in the heavens above, or in the earth beneath, or in the waters under the earth, can be compared to it".[18]

For the remainder of the century, users of Ludgate Hill Station had to endure the long, narrow, windswept platforms, the draughty staircases, and the all-pervading gloom. Reconstruction eventually began in 1907, but by the time it was completed in 1910 the cross-London steam suburban services which it had accommodated were in decline. Closure finally came in 1929.[19]

Inner Circle: Sulphurous Gloom

From the LCDR Extension Line at Ludgate Hill it was but a short and noisy ride through smoke-filled tunnels to either Aldersgate Street or Farringdon Street on the Inner Circle (Met and MDR). Even if, by 1871, the novelty of an underground railway was beginning to wear off, its particular characteristics and unique contribution to rail travel in London remained. The line and its stations continued to attract comment, favourable and otherwise. As much of this relates to the Inner Circle as a whole rather than to individual stations, the line is considered here in its entirety.

The sulphurous, soot-laden atmosphere of a steam-worked underground railway made a lasting impression on railway workers and passengers alike. The staff, it was said, found beards useful as filters. Despite the provision of ventilation shafts and the cutting of "blow-holes" in the tunnel roof, the air remained thick. In response to complaints, the Met took the unlikely position that the fumes were beneficial to health, especially for those with asthma and bronchial conditions, while the sulphuric acid present in the tunnels acted as a disinfectant![20] Needless to say, these claims failed to convince the travelling public (or the staff):

---

18. *SLP* 22.6.1889
19. *Railway Magazine* Dec.1964
20. White p. 84; Barker & Robbins pp. 125, 235–237

Occasional passengers complain of headaches, sulphurous taste on the palate, and a stinging sensation in the throat.... The employees at the station [King's Cross] *complain of the air, affirming that no man whose lungs are delicate can keep at work without suffering, and that a short dry, hacking cough is common among all who are on duty.*

A coroner inquiring into the death from suffocation of a female passenger at King's Cross admitted that "he avoided the railway as much as possible, because of the depressing effect he experienced from the confined atmosphere".[21] A contributor to the *English Illustrated Magazine* who had taken a footplate ride round the Inner Circle in 1893 described the atmosphere between King's Cross and Edgware Road as "on a par with the 'tween decks, forrud' of a modern ironclad in bad weather... By the time we reached Gower Street I was coughing and spluttering like a boy with his first cigar".[22] It was at Gower Street, in 1873, that the Met had attempted to ventilate the station by drawing air from the tube of the Pneumatic Despatch Company which crossed the line at that point on its way to Holborn. The pneumatic tube had been opened in 1865 to carry Post Office mail, but owing to technical problems it ceased operation in 1874, depriving the Met of its source of ventilation.[23]

In a successful attempt to improve conditions on the southern part of the Inner Circle, the MDR provided tunnel shaft ventilators along the embankment; a proposal by the Metropolitan Board of Works to remove them in 1883, evidently on aesthetic grounds, was greeted by railway passengers with derision: "Are we, who are the millions, to be smothered or choked in the underground railway because a few loungers on the embankment object to the ventilators?"[24]

The problem of foul air on the Inner Circle persisted throughout the late Victorian period. In 1897 a report of a committee appointed by the Board of Trade to inquire into the ventilation of the underground railway observed that, while the installation of fans would help to alleviate the problem, they would be expensive, and unwelcome too if they discharged fumes at street level. The only satisfactory remedy, concluded the committee, would be electric traction.[25] That of course would come to the Inner Circle, but not until the opening years of the twentieth century.

To an American visitor to London, writing in the *Toledo Blade* in 1877, the underground railway was a revelation, far exceeding expectations. From his description of the stations, he appears not to have travelled on the more enclosed and poorly ventilated section between King's Cross and Edgware Road:

I had figured to myself a dark, narrow, dismal tunnel, where the passengers were annoyed with smoke and breathe the damps of the tomb; but I found

---

21. *New York Tribune* quoted in Emmerson p. 63
22. Reprinted in *Railway Magazine* May–June 1944
23. *RFS* Feb.1874
24. *SLP* 23.6.1883, 30.6.1883
25. *ROG* Oct.1897

*that I was very greatly mistaken. The descent from the street is by a broad
and easy stairway which lands you in a pleasant and spacious depot [sic]
roofed over with glass to admit the light and to exclude the rain. Here you
can walk about or sit and read your paper while waiting for the train, or
you can amuse yourself by reading the advertising bills which are posted
on the walls.*[26]

Certainly the glazed, overall-roofed stations of the Met and MDR were spacious and
impressive, despite the soot-blackened brickwork of the retaining walls lining the cuttings
in which the stations were situated.

Our American visitor would probably have been less impressed by Edgware Road
Station, the subject of an extended essay in the *Indicator* in 1883:

*Edgware Road Station is shrouded in gloom of a dispiriting and
disheartening kind of a character in common with other Metropolitan
Railway stations, but hardly so dark as the majority of them. Its interior
arrangements, besides the murky atmosphere, are pretty much like those
of other underground stations eastward and westward.*

Having visited the signal box and locomotive sheds, the writer continues:

*The underground regions of Edgware Road Station possess a variety of
aspects and atmospheres, that must be seen and breathed to be appreciated,
for there is a tunnel so black that nothing can be seen but the white lights
of the fast-approaching engine, with air loaded with smoky emanations,
while there are semi-darkness, and open air, thinly wreathed with smoke
and bright sunlight, serving to make the gloom of the distant tunnel more
obvious, and the half or quarter light of the enclosed platforms more
tantalising.*[27]

The writer has put into words some of the sights and sensations of the underground
railway that were familiar to countless late Victorian travellers, but rarely articulated by
them. A similar response to the underground experience, albeit from the viewpoint of the
footplate, comes from the contributor to the *English Illustrated Magazine* in 1893, whom
we left coughing and spluttering in the smoke-laden air of Gower Street Station. Here he is
approaching Blackfriars:

*Far off in the distance was a small square-shaped hole, seemingly high up
in the air, and from it came four silver threads palpitating like gossamers*

---

26.   Quoted in *RSOG* June 1877
27.   Quoted in *ROG* Aug.1883

*in the morning breeze. Larger and larger grew the hole, the threads
became rails, and the hole a station, Blackfriars, with rays of golden
sunlight piercing through the gloom.*

The writer continues to capture the other-worldliness of the steam-worked Inner Circle
as the train approaches Mark Lane Station:

*...where ghostly-looking figures paced a hidden platform across which
fell great golden beams that looked like impassable barriers. Yet, ere one
could take a second glance, the beams were riven asunder and a black
engine blotted them out with clouds of writhing steam.*[28]

So back down to earth now, and the practicalities of information and signage available
to passengers using the Inner Circle. These varied according to whether the station was
a Met or MDR responsibility. Tickets were generally checked on entry to the platforms,
and passengers were informed of the correct platform for their direction of travel (also
indicated by an overstamp on the ticket). At some stations small indicators, placed close to
the platform entrance, showed the destination of the next train. These were operated by the
official checking tickets.

Stations served by Met trains displayed hanging signs above the platforms indicating
where each class of carriage stopped, train formations being standardised. For passengers
arriving by train the name of the station would be called out by porters, but as we have
found elsewhere their pronunciation was not impeccable: Glawster Rowd, Victaw-ia,
Menshun Ouse and Mawgit Street were among the cries encountered.[29]

Clapham Junction: Bewildering Enigma

Railway junctions, it was sometimes said, were a necessary evil. The interlocking of
different railway companies' lines at one location, though a source of confusion to some,
offered substantial benefits to many. With the growing elaboration of the railway system in
late Victorian times, junctions where passengers could interchange between one line and
another became indispensable. And in the London area, Clapham Junction (LSWR and
LBSCR) could claim to be the most indispensable of all.

The difficulties facing the user of Clapham Junction as an interchange – especially the
unfamiliar user – were captured well in a word sketch published in *Chambers's Journal* in
1873. These are extracts from imaginary conversations between passengers and railway
officials:

---

28.   Reprinted in *Railway Magazine* May–June 1944
29.   Emmerson pp. 70–71

> *"Clapham Junction! Change here for Chatham and Dover line."*
> *"Guard, does this train go on?" "No. All change here."*
> *"Which is the way to the Crystal Palace train?" "Down the steps, along the tunnel, and up the fourth passage to the right."*
> *"This train for Victoria?" "No, you should have gone up the stairs on the other side of the tunnel. This is the down platform."*
> *"Porter, they told me this was the main line platform, but I can't see the Brighton train."*
> *"This is the main line of the South-Western. You've come up the wrong stairs."*
> *"Oh bother! I never can find the right stairs at this place. The other day I was in Croydon when I thought I was going to Waterloo." "We can't help it sir. You should have read the names of the lines and stations as you went through the tunnel."*

A commentator on the sketch claimed that this was no exaggeration, and anyone who really knew Clapham Junction "must have experienced the pursuit of knowledge under difficulties". The porter was quite right to say that he and his fellow servants could not help it. They did their best to assist bewildered passengers, but the bewilderment still occurred:

> *Imagine Mrs. Brown walking through a semi-dark tunnel, looking up eight or nine flights of those steps, through eight or nine openings at the sides of the tunnel, and hopelessly reading, or attempting to read, the names of four or five railway companies, and of a number of stations varying in distance from two to two hundred miles.*[30]

As these words were being written, work was beginning on the rebuilding and simplification of Clapham Junction. The first part to be done was the LBSCR side of the station; the works included a new access to platforms from a "long gallery across the line", a new booking office and waiting rooms, a spacious refreshment room, and four new platforms.[31]

The work proceeded rapidly, and was completed during April 1874. The new station frontage to the LBSCR platforms was a long, low building of white brick with stone facings, but its appearance was greeted with immense disappointment:

> *The general appearance of the station, viewed from either side, forcibly reminds one of an Indian bungalow and backwood "shanty" combined... Anything less effective, with a view to an ornate and pleasing design, it is hard to imagine.*

---

30. *SLP* 3.1.1874
31. *SLP* 10.1.1874

It was greatly regretted that the LBSCR and LSWR had not worked together to produce a uniform design, "but it is not too late to hope that the new building which will take the place of the comfortless South-Western station will be a standing protest against the wretchedly inharmonious erection which is to do duty for the sister company". Work on the LSWR buildings took longer than on the LBSCR side, but it was generally agreed that the results were better.[32]

That was not the end of the problems at Clapham Junction. Although the inadequate buildings had been replaced, the station continued to be approached through dirty, narrow passages where "frequent scuffles took place, and the public... were threatened with actual danger to life and limb". One of the approaches was obstructed by tram horses entering and leaving adjoining stables. For a station handling 1,500 trains a day, and between 1,000 and 3,000 passengers an hour, the conditions, said the Battersea Vestry, were just not good enough.[33]

ENTRANCE TO CLAPHAM JUNCTION STATION.

ANDOE-ROAD ENTRANCE AND THE MINIATURE MONT BLANC.

THE TUNNEL, OR SHOOTING GALLERY.

32.   *SLP* 28.3.1874, 16.5.1874, 8.8.1874, 21.11.1874
33.   *SLP* 25.5.1889

In 1889 a spirited journalist took up the cause of Clapham Junction:

> *A fearsome place is Clapham Junction – a bewildering, misleading,*
> *heart-breaking railway enigma – a puzzle made up of many platforms,*
> *innumerable and mysterious recesses, narrow entrances – a paved Mont*
> *Blanc in miniature, and a perforated tunnel of the most unique description.*

Clapham Junction, he said, like Topsy, had just growed, or been "junctioned into existence by degrees".

His strongest condemnation was reserved for the so-called "Falcon" entrance – the one shared with tramway horses, with a stable on one side and a farrier's forge on the other. Accompanied by a cartoon in which top-hatted passengers do battle with tram horses, the writer claims that "in no other country in the world, and at no other station in the world, could such a sight – so uniquely nasty and horrible – be seen".

The Junction's most famous feature was the tunnel or "shooting gallery" linking the platform staircases:

> *...as a puzzle, as a railway conundrum, as a thing of mystery, as a happy*
> *hunting-ground for scrimmages, confusion, and bad language, it occupies*
> *an altogether exceptionally proud position! It has more terrors for old ladies*
> *than the rate-collector or a beggar with his foot in the doorway; and perhaps*
> *at no other junction have so many people lost themselves and their tempers.*

The "Mont Blanc in miniature" turns out to be a steeply sloping passage from the tunnel to the cab stand and the principal up platform for Vauxhall and Waterloo. A notice at the summit informs passengers that "this bell rings for a train to Vauxhall and Waterloo from No.3 Platform":

> *It often happens, when the platform is crowded with persons waiting for an*
> *up-train, that the tinkle of the bell is heard. Down the steep incline rushes*
> *the mob of anxious, eager passengers, the accelerated pace through the*
> *rapid descent causing numerous accidents and many absurd situations.*

A familiar story? Remember Willesden Junction, Loughborough Junction, and the old Waterloo?

The piece concludes with a catalogue of the many retail, commercial and community developments taking place at the time around Clapham Junction Station – an extension to the Falcon Tavern, a new food distribution warehouse, a new bank, a new public hall, a new drapery store (Arding and Hobbs), a new free library: "It is surely time for our old friend Clapham Junction to wake up – to do something more for the public than merely take its coppers".[34]

---

34.   *SLP* 29.6.1889

Three years later, in 1892, passenger deputations to the LBSCR and LSWR demanded improvements to the "wretched condition of the approaches" to the station, but the companies were unable to offer a speedy remedy.[35] Four years further on, and John Burns, MP for Battersea, was pressing for similar improvements. But passengers and tram horses still ran the daily risk of collision – one of "the many inconveniences, sanitary and otherwise", abounding in the vicinity of the station.[36]

Finsbury Park: Paradise Lost

Just at the time that Clapham Junction was undergoing reconstruction, in 1874, so, north of the Thames, was Finsbury Park. What had started life in 1861 as a simple, two-platform wayside halt known as Seven Sisters Road was growing into a major interchange for GNR suburban passengers. It had been renamed Finsbury Park in 1869. Its importance would be considerably enhanced in 1875 with the opening of the Canonbury Spur to the North London Railway and Broad Street Station.

The 1874 reconstruction was thorough. It comprised a 400-foot long frontage, and new booking and parcels offices, a cloakroom and waiting rooms on the ground floor. A spacious subway, lined with tiles, gave access to staircases to the four island platforms, each served by a luggage lift. The platforms were equipped with first and second class waiting rooms and staff accommodation.[37]

Four years later the *Railway Sheet and Official Gazette* carried an article on the station, written by a season ticket holder. The author claims that, with the possible exception of Clapham Junction, Finsbury Park "has given greater evidence of extraordinary development than any [other] place in the suburbs of London". A bold claim, but Finsbury Park does illustrate, in railway terms, the truth of the words "tall oaks from little acorns grow".

Whereas the single porter employed at the original wooden station of 1861 had ample time to cultivate the grassy banks below the lineside hawthorn hedge, the porter of 1878 has:

> ...hardly time to think, wanted on this platform and on that, his eyes almost continually on signals to see what train is coming next, worried by a thousand questions, agitated by late comers and perverse travellers who will go wrong, and his innumerable duties connected with the work of the station. What time has he to cultivate banks; and, alas, where are the banks?

The arrival of W.H. Smith's bookstall at the station is recorded. Originally the morning papers were obtained from an "industrious local" who hovered near the station entrance. Then "Smith the irrepressible" arrived, first with a trestle table served by a small boy with

35.   *BST* 16.1.1892
36.   *South Western Star* 28.2.1896
37.   *RFS* Aug.1874

a paper knife, then by a portable stall which increased in size as trade improved – as "the growth of a station is indicated by the appearance and size of its bookstall".

Little by little the station was transformed from a country halt into a busy junction – stone steps in place of sloping footpaths, an iron footbridge in place of a level foot crossing, more trains and more passengers. The opening of the Highgate and Edgware line in 1867, and the Alexandra Palace branch in 1873, were milestones in the process of growth. And so to the complete rebuilding of 1874 and – sure sign of progress – a large W.H. Smith bookstall "and a supplementary stand below, with boys scouring the neighbourhood, delivering papers, & c".

By 1878 average daily ordinary ticket sales had reached around 3,000, and there were about 500 stopping trains a day – still a long way behind Clapham Junction, but a massive increase in a few short years. Finsbury Park "is rapidly becoming one of the most popular suburbs of the North of London, because its means of access to and from are of the most complete kind":

> Greybeards may sigh over the departed sweet scented zephyrs, the rural glories of wood and water; but the practical materialist of today surveys the pasture land of the past from the standpoint of his bank book and chuckles over the result; rejoicing that "Finsbury Park" has developed from a signal box to a junction.[38]

Most of the complaints made about the new Finsbury Park Station were relatively minor. In 1876, two years after its completion, a journalist claimed that the station was "noted for its draughts and discomforts", but no precise details are given.[39] Of more concern to some passengers was the practice of coating the exteriors of the cast iron stoves in the waiting rooms with "some oleaginous compound" at the beginning of winter,

> ...the consequence of which is that the poor passengers who resort with increased readiness to these rooms as a refuge from the biting blasts which have suddenly succeeded the genial autumn weather, find them filled with the stifling fumes which the fires in the stoves naturally produce in attacking the combustible element which has thus been placed within their reach.

It took several days for the greasy coating to burn off. The same problem seems to have occurred at other GNR suburban stations.[40]

One problem that Finsbury Park passengers shared with those of Clapham Junction was the poor provision of information as to which trains left from which platforms. The matter was discussed at a meeting of the Hornsey District Council in January 1897; it was

---

38. *RSOG* July 1878
39. *North Metropolitan & Holloway Press* 21.10.1876
40. *HFPJ* 14.11.1884

alleged that, even for the regular traveller, the situation was "confusion worse confounded". The provision of an indicator had been raised with the general manager of the GNR, who had replied:

> *...it is somewhat difficult to find an efficient indicator owing to the number*
> *of destinations to be covered, and the fact that a good many of the trains*
> *miss certain stations. It is... essential that the indicator should not in any*
> *way prove misleading to the public.*

Nine months passed by and nothing was done. A correspondent considered that all that was required was some determination and mechanical ingenuity. "Other railway companies, notably the Metropolitan, indicate the route of each one of their many trains, while the Great Eastern have quite a number of contrivances for serving the same end."[41]

At last, in July 1898, it was reported that "a large semaphore sign post has been fixed on the platform, and passengers from Finsbury Park can now see for themselves where to entrain without being under the necessity of apologetically asking a porter or unctuous station master to condescend to inform them". The precise nature of the "semaphore sign post", and whether one was provided on every platform, is not revealed. One hopes that it applied to the NLR trains, however, as it was claimed that these were labelled on one side only, so that in one direction passengers could not see the labels without clambering across the rails! The indicator would also have been of service to passengers requiring a stopping train to Harringay, Hornsey and Wood Green, generally announced by the Finsbury Park platform porter as the train for "Arringhornoodgreen". "Unless you happen to know the line", remarked a user of the station, "you might fancy you were somewhere in the Highlands".[42]

---

41. *HFPJ* 23.1.1897, 11.9.1897
42. *North Middlesex Chronicle* 16.7.1898

CHAPTER 6

TRAINS

Discomfort and Dust

Short wheelbase non-gangwayed compartment carriages with slam doors to each compartment were universal on London's metropolitan and suburban railways in the late Victorian period. The era of open saloon carriages with roomier accommodation for standing passengers had yet to come, and it was not until the turn of the century that voices in their favour began to be heard. In 1901 a contributor to the *Railway Magazine* was "inclined to think that the evil [of overcrowding] is certainly aggravated by our British 'compartment' system; whatever advantages compartments may have for through express journeys, they are most unsuitable for short 'omnibus' traffic".[1] But that was a minority view at the time, and most railway companies clung tenaciously to compartment carriages for suburban traffic well into the twentieth century.

Four-wheeled carriages with rudimentary suspension and braking running on jointed track could never have provided a wholly smooth and quiet ride. But by and large passengers tolerated the bumpy motion, uneven braking and acceleration, and rhythmic rail noise as unavoidable features of rail travel. Comments on riding quality were usually restricted to comparisons between one company's carriages and another's.

In 1881 a regular traveller between Victoria and Ludgate Hill compared the GNR trains on that line unfavourably with those of the LCDR:

> *The frequent jerks on leaving a station, and the sudden stoppages, with bumps, &c., are very trying to nervous persons. ...To travel after by a London, Chatham, and Dover train is simply heavenly, and quite a luxury.*

Although the GNR carriages were better appointed internally, their sharp braking system did cause some discomfort.[2] Later in the century, however, the position seems to have been reversed: a traveller from New Southgate to King's Cross regularly changed from a GNR train to an LCDR train at Finsbury Park; the brakes on the latter were so fierce that

---

1. *Railway Magazine* July 1901
2. *SLP* 17.12.1881

"you found yourself thrown out of your seat on to your fellow-passenger opposite".[3]

In a soot-laden, smoke-filled atmosphere, keeping carriage interiors clean was an uphill task. Dirty windows, dusty floors and smutty upholstery were all too common. But again standards varied. An LSWR passenger who thought the condition of that company's carriages would bear improvement had a rude awakening when travelling on another (unspecified) company's line: "the state of the carriage I rode in... was simply awful. It required all my philosophy to enable me to sit out a short journey of about twenty minutes". His experience had been shared, on another occasion, by an elderly gentleman travelling on the same railway. So disgusted was he at the filthy state of the compartment in which he was sitting that he pulled the communication cord. When approached by the guard he said: "unaccustomed as I am to travelling in a pig sty you will have the goodness to show me into a clean carriage before you proceed". The guard acquiesced, the train restarted, and no more was heard of the matter.[4]

So long as carriages were kept reasonably clean, their external appearance mattered little to the Victorian traveller, and the choice of livery had as much to do with durability as with company identity. However, it is worth recording the colour schemes that would have been familiar to regular passengers.

By the end of the nineteenth century six companies (GER, GNR, LCDR, LTSR, Met and NLR) had adopted a teak finish for their carriages. Five more had chosen varying shades of brown – the LBSCR and MDR as an overall finish, the GWR, LNWR and LSWR in combination with lighter colours above the waistline. The remaining companies (MR and SER) used lake or maroon. There were some exceptions to the rule – for example, the Met used white paint above the waistline on its first class carriages, and the LNWR chose varnished teak for its Outer Circle stock because of its ability to withstand the damaging effects of smoke-filled tunnels.

The subdued liveries of most of the rolling stock matched the predominantly grimy surroundings in which it operated, though a splash of colour could be introduced by a clean locomotive with bright paintwork and polished brass; engines appeared in a variety of colours, the most popular being green.[5]

Class Distinctions

Late Victorian society was deeply class conscious, and the railway companies responded by providing segregated accommodation on their trains. Most companies offered first, second and third class compartments, even on local and metropolitan trains, although the NLR did not provide third class until 1875. In an interview for the *Railway Magazine* in 1898, the general manager of the NLR explained why his company had differed in this respect:

3.   *Palmers Green & Southgate Gazette* 23.5.1930
4.   *RTT* 1.6.1889
5.   Sekon pp. 182, 199; *North London Railway: A Pictorial Record* (1979) p. xv

As a matter of fact the character of people travelling by the North London Railway has altered a great deal. For 25 years after the railway was opened our passengers were all of a class that could afford to travel first or second class, but as the districts we serve became more thickly populated, another class of travellers came to us, and the directors quickly recognised the need of third-class accommodation. [6]

Although the general manager did not say so, the decision was not unconnected with the fact that, in 1875, the NLR started running trains over GNR lines in north London, the GNR trains on those lines already carrying third class passengers. Also in 1875 the MR introduced

THAT IT SHOULD COME TO THIS!

Boy. " Second-class, sir ? "
Captain. " I nevah travel second-class ! "
Boy. " This way third, sir ! "

---

6.   *Railway Magazine* Sept.1898

a service between Moorgate Street and Richmond via Cricklewood and Gunnersbury. This conveyed first and third class accommodation only, and could have attracted second class passengers away from the NLR trains to Richmond if the latter had not offered third class.[7] In fact, the MR took the surprising step of abolishing second class altogether from the beginning of 1875; other companies with more extensive suburban services felt unable to do this because of the potential loss of second class revenue from regular passengers switching to third class.[8]

Railway companies made some effort to ensure that first class passengers received preferential service – for example by marshalling first class carriages near the centre of the train where platform canopies would afford protection from the weather.[9] In 1883 the LCDR was commended for placing third class carriages at the front of the train, thereby preventing third class passengers from blocking part of the Ludgate Hill platform nearest the staircase, "to the inconvenience of first and second class passengers".[10] The discipline seems to have loosened, however, for in 1892 it was claimed that "the officials of the London, Chatham and Dover Railway persist in making up their trains so that no one knows at which end is the class of carriage for which he has taken a ticket".[11]

Complaints were continually made about the shortage of carriages of one class or another. In 1874 users of Loughborough Junction (LCDR) criticised the shortage of first and second class carriages on trains to the City.[12] At a public meeting arranged by the South of London Railway Passengers' Protection Association in February 1883, users voiced their demand for more third class carriages on the LCDR and LBSCR; only "nobs and snobs" rode in first class carriages, they said.[13] Richmond passengers were similarly concerned, in 1889, that there was an over-provision of first class accommodation on the LSWR trains to Waterloo, and that the second and third class were "lamentably insufficient".[14]

Differences in the quality of accommodation between the three classes were usually substantial. The MDR stock of 1871, for example, comprised first class carriages with four spacious and well-upholstered compartments, second class carriages with five rather less generously proportioned and equipped compartments, and third class carriages with five basic compartments furnished with a strip of carpet on each seat and a padded back strip at shoulder height. All these carriages seated five a side in each compartment.[15] New carriages introduced on the Met in 1872 were, according to Edward Walford, "luxuriously fitted up" in first class to carry sixty passengers, whereas the second and third class carriages accommodated at least eighty.[16] GNR suburban carriages of the 1880s were described as "austere in decoration", even in first class.[17]

---

7.   Sekon p. 181
8.   Nock pp.69 70
9.   Course p. 257
10. *SLP* 10.2.1883
11. *BST* 6.8.1892
12. *SLP* 5.9.1874, 17.10.1874
13. *SLP* 3.2.1883
14. *RTT* 4.5.1889
15. Lee C, *One Hundred Years of the District* (1968) pp. 12–13
16. Walford p. 228
17. Nock p. 76

On the SER, third class carriages earned a reputation for their spartan interiors, which

> *...took the form of a cheerless bare rectangular box with hard wooden*
> *seats and "half-way" partitions separating the compartments. The*
> *partitions were so low that when the passenger sat down with his back to*
> *one of them, his head nearly collided with the back hair and best hat of*
> *the female in the next compartment.*[18]

Whilst acknowledging that the SER's third class carriages were the worst of all, a commentator in 1892 considered that those on the LCDR came a close second for discomfort, and accused the general manager of talking nonsense "when he said that after all they were not so bad that people could not or would not travel in them"![19]

The "half-way" partitions in third class carriages were not limited to the SER. They were the cause of an amusing incident observed on the Met in 1894. Two ladies, sitting back-to-back, were wearing enormous netted buns. During the journey the buns came so close together that a sword pin in one of the ladies' hats caught the bun net of the other. Neither noticed until one rose to alight, when "she was considerably astonished at finding that her head had a decided objection to being moved, and the other lady was equally surprised at finding her head wanting to move without her consent". Another lady in the carriage came to the rescue and released the entanglement. "Perhaps", concluded a witness to the incident, "those ladies will now see the absurdity and danger of wearing unnecessary appendages".[20]

More Light than Heat

The earliest railway carriages were lit by oil, and oil roof-lamps continued in use on some London lines well into the late Victorian period. But gas lighting, in the form of fish-tail jet burners in globes, had been available since the 1860s. The first railway in Britain to use gas regularly was the NLR, which introduced a system of low pressure coal gas lighting in 1862. The gas containers were carried in the brakevan of each train, and from 1865 were replenished at the Broad Street terminus.[21] In September 1876 an explosion occurred at Broad Street when the gas bags of an NLR train were being refilled, causing "temporary pandemonium" but no casualties.[22]

On the Met, the gas was carried in rubber bags secured within wooden boxes in the carriage roofs:

> *The light thus afforded to the passengers is so bright as to utterly remove*
> *all sense of travelling underground, and entirely dissipate that nervousness*

---

18.   E.L. Ahrons quoted in Course pp. 246–247
19.   *BST* 6.8.1892
20.   *Kilburn Times* 24.2.1894
21.   Course p. 250; Sekon pp. 166–167; *North London Railway: A Pictorial Record* (1979) p. xv
22.   *North Metropolitan & Holloway Press* 23.9.1876

which the semi-obscurity of ordinary oil-lighted railway carriages gives
to the sensitive during their transit through the tunnels on other lines.[23]

Less well pleased with the light fittings on the Met was the laundress who, in 1870, was injured by a falling carriage lamp; she was awarded twenty pounds damages from the railway company.[24]

In the late 1870s the Pintsch system of compressed oil gas was introduced; this provided more effective and longer lasting illumination. The LNWR and Met had both tried it successfully by 1877, the MDR adopted it in 1878,[25] and the LSWR followed in 1879. "As far as I am able to judge", wrote an LSWR passenger, "the new oil gaslight is, though small, remarkably bright and clear; it does not smell, and does not become dull or go out".[26] A similar system, supplied by Pope's Patent Lighting Company, was in use in 1883 on GWR trains running on the Inner Circle:

One jet in the middle of each compartment gives ample lighting power,
and obviates the frequent damage to hats arising from the two lamps
hitherto in use close to the doors.[27]

The NLR, having pioneered coal gas lighting, now found itself left behind; in 1882 a third class passenger complained that there were but "two miserable lights in each carriage, equal to one penny candle".[28]

Introduction of the incandescent mantle in the late 1880s improved the quality of gas lighting in carriages, as it did at stations, but standards remained variable. A GNR season ticket holder complained in 1888 that "perhaps there is no line which uses a greater variety of lamps than the Great Northern, and certainly none which gives less light to its passengers".[29] The writer commented on the large number of tunnels through which GNR trains passed in the London area, and the consequent necessity to have gas lights on during daylight hours. In fact the GNR, in common with other companies, issued detailed instructions to guards and station staff as to when carriage gas lighting should be turned up or down during the course of a journey.[30]

Although experiments with electric carriage lighting took place in the early 1880s, railway companies were slow to adopt it. In January 1884 the MDR fitted one train on its Putney Bridge line with an electric lighting installation. The current was generated by a small steam engine and dynamo in the brakevan. The carriages were lit by twenty-eight incandescent lamps of twenty candle-power each, giving "a very brilliant light".[31]

23.   Walford pp. 228–229 quoting a brochure of 1865
24.   *Illustrated London News* 12.2.1870
25.   *RSOG* March 1877; Lee C, *One Hundred Years of the District* (1968) p. 13
26.   *RTT* 6.12.1879
27.   *ROG* May 1883
28.   *Hackney & Kingsland Gazette* 17.5.1882
29.   *IG* 27.8.1888
30.   GNR Appendix to Working Timetables etc. (1905)
31.   *ROG* Jan.1884

Successful though the experiment was claimed to be, the MDR thereafter turned its attention to the provision of electric reading lamps for its passengers, as an addition to, not in replacement of, the existing gas lights. Following a successful trial in 1892, the MDR contracted with the Railway Electric Reading Lamp Company for the installation of up to 10,000 reading lamps in its carriages. In every compartment four lamps were placed under the hat rails, each with a small machine into which the passenger was required to insert a penny; at the press of a button electric light was delivered for half an hour.[32] A shaded reflector could be adjusted by the passenger.

"Good gracious! In this great Victorian era what can we not get for one penny, even within the precincts of a railway platform?" asked a newspaper columnist. His penny would buy a railway ticket, scent for a pocket handkerchief, cough sweets, wax vestas or a local newspaper "and, Great Scott! to crown all... a pennyworth of electric light by which to enjoy all the other pennyworths. Of a truth this is a wonderful world".[33] The editor of the *Railway Herald* was less impressed, however:

> *Why passengers who desire to read in a train should have to provide their own light we don't exactly understand. That carriages can be efficiently and even brilliantly illuminated has long been demonstrated by the Midland Company, whose suburban trains are lighted by means of two gas lamps in each compartment.*[34]

When, eventually, the railway companies were persuaded that electric carriage lighting was best, the system developed by Stone's of Deptford in 1894 was widely employed. Two of the London railway companies, the LCDR and LTSR, retained oil-lit carriages until they were ready to adopt electric lighting.[35]

Built-in carriage heating was virtually non-existent on suburban trains in the nineteenth century; warm clothing and the body heat of fellow passengers had to suffice. Foot warmers, usually filled with hot water, were available at certain stations, but these were intended for longer journeys; on the GNR, for example, the nearest station to London that had them (apart from King's Cross) was Hatfield. On-train heating had to await the arrival of steam radiators under the seats, fed from the locomotive.[36]

During the summer, over-heated carriages could be a problem. Curtains were sometimes provided in first class compartments; in 1874 a south London passenger requested, in vain, that they should be fitted in second and third class also.[37] By the end of the century blinds were being fitted to the seat windows on many carriages, but for at least one LSWR passenger that did not go far enough:

---

32.   Emmerson p. 68
33.   *BST* 3.9.1892
34.   *Railway Herald* 21.10.1893
35.   Course p. 250
36.   Course p. 251, GNR Appendix to Working Timetables etc. (1905)
37.   *SLP* 31.1.1874

It is a pretty generally accepted fact that the sun which shines on the seat windows of a railway train is practically certain to shine on the door windows as well. No doubt this did not occur to the South-Western Railway Company when they were having their rolling stock made. ...In the hot weather any improvement of a kind which ensures that a whole carriage will be shady instead of only two-thirds of it will excite a large share of gratitude.[38]

For Smokers... and Ladies Only

Under the Regulation of Railways Act, 1868, smoking carriages of any particular class were required to be included in all trains conveying more than one carriage of that class, but the Met and MDR secured exemptions as their lines were underground. None of the railway companies favoured smoking because of possible damage to their property, but they recognised that money was to be made from selling tobacco in refreshment rooms and leasing platform space to the owners of slot machines.[39]

Workman (politely, to old lady, who has accidentally got into a smoking compartment). "You don't object to my pipe, I 'ope, mum?"
Old Lady. "Yes, I *do* object, very strongly!"
Workman. "Oh! Then out you get!!"

38. *RTT* 20.5.1899
39. Course pp. 248–249

The exemptions secured by the underground companies were unpopular. In its defence, the Met argued that ladies would dislike using its trains if, at times, they found themselves in a smoking compartment. A few passengers who defied the ban were taken to court and fined, but many smokers escaped without penalty, especially in third class carriages. The Met's claim that the prohibition safeguarded the interests of female passengers was undermined by the fact that many women and girls were prepared to travel third class in the company of smokers who transgressed with impunity. "No, the Company are composed of ladies' men who fear to discommode their first-class female passengers", cried the *West London Observer*.[40]

At a public meeting of passengers at Hammersmith in May 1871 it was agreed that smoking should be encouraged rather than obstructed, as the Met "had a nasty habit of giving free carriage to stinking fish and other feverable and offensive things that made the fragrant weed a necessity". The matter became the subject of a petition to the House of Commons signed by residents of Hammersmith and neighbouring districts. This pointed out that some journeys on the Met lasted longer than journeys by the main line companies, which were obliged to provide smoking accommodation.[41]

The Met persisted in its policy of showing up the few as an example to the many by employing so-called "pipers" to travel on the trains and apprehend smokers – a practice condemned as "un-English" and "discreditable to the company". The reaction of some smokers to the activities of these "pipers" is evident from a case that came before the Marylebone Police Court in October 1871. The "piper" on this occasion was a Met travelling inspector who one morning boarded the 8.05 train from Hammersmith to the City. The defendant, and several others, entered the same compartment as the inspector and began to smoke after the train had started. At each station the defendant beckoned to friends on the platform whom he knew to be smokers to get into the same compartment. He even had a carriage key, and locked the door against any non-smokers who tried to board. By the time the train reached Farringdon Street there were about fifteen smokers in the compartment, which, not surprisingly, was "filled with smoke" (mostly pipe smoke, it appears). The unfortunate inspector was not only asphyxiated but also ridiculed, as the defendant called him a "spy" in front of the other passengers. The episode resulted in a fine of twenty-two shillings, but the smokers had made an emphatic protest.[42]

The ban on smoking on the Met and MDR was further undermined by the fact that trains of other companies which had smoking carriages travelled over the same lines and served the same stations. Eventually the two underground companies bowed to the inevitable and from 1st September 1874 provided smoking accommodation on their trains.[43] The provision was not universally welcomed, however, as one commentator observed:

---

40.   *West London Observer* 4.3.1871
41.   *West London Observer* 6.5.1871, 13.5.1871
42.   *West London Observer* 21.10.1871
43.   Lee C, *The Metropolitan Line* (1972) pp. 19–20; Lee (MDR) pp. 35–36

The Metropolitan lines are peculiar. The trains are so numerous, and the influx of passengers is so capricious, that it is almost impossible to provide accommodation in two kinds. People have often to rush into any carriage which offers itself, and the supply is not infrequently short, so that ladies and others averse to smoking will, under the new régime, *often be compelled to submit to a nuisance they would avoid.*[44]

Just short of two months after the ban had been lifted the same commentator claimed that the trains had become "pervaded with the odour of stale tobacco" as "the smokers practically do as they like... the most inveterate smoker might surely abstain ten minutes or a quarter of an hour; and there are few who can plead that these brief journeys afford their only time for a smoke".[45]

Other companies too faced problems in enforcing smoking restrictions. The LCDR had particular difficulties with its third class passengers, who, when confronted with overcrowded carriages, simply occupied whatever seats they could find; the result was that smokers smoked in non-smoking compartments and non-smokers travelled in smoking compartments, causing maximum discomfort to all non-smokers.[46]

Whereas smokers on the Met had made their protest by creating a suffocating atmosphere in one compartment, smokers on the LSWR sought relief from such conditions:

In Germany, possibly, ten natives of that country would feel they had reached the highest summit of earthly felicity when cooped up in a small compartment with closed windows and filled with a volume of smoke so dense that one could almost lean one's back against it. But the average Englishman... prefers to smoke his pipe or cigar on his journey from town after a hard day's work or a night's pleasure, without the risk of suffocation.

Remedies suggested to the LSWR were to limit the number of passengers in smoking compartments to eight, and to improve ventilation.[47] The former is unlikely to have eased the overcrowding problem, but the latter deserved consideration.

The need for better ventilation of smoking compartments was widely recognised but less easily achieved. Some of the most stifling conditions were found in third class smoking carriages on the NLR. "For a dose of double-distilled condensed and concentrated essence of common shag", said one observer, "give me a third-class smoker on the North London. You could cut the smoke with a knife, and poison your mother-in-law with it". It was, he said, "the peculiar habit of smokers to close the carriage windows". The remedy,

---

44. *SLP* 12.9.1874
45. *SLP* 24.10.1874
46. *Camberwell News* 23.12.1876
47. *RTT* 6.4.1889

A SIMPLE DEVICE ENABLING SMOKERS TO SMOKE IN NON-SMOKING
COMPARTMENTS WITHOUT ANNOYANCE TO THE OTHER PASSENGERS

SAFEGUARDING
THE
PROPRIETIES

he suggested, was to have chimneys on the carriage roofs, the upward draught creating a tolerably clear atmosphere.[48]

For what may have been the most curious encounter between a smoking and non-smoking passenger we return to the underground railway. Towards the end of 1892 a gentleman was sitting alone in a first class smoking compartment on the Inner Circle enjoying a cigarette. Just as the train was about to leave Victoria a lady hurriedly entered the compartment with a small dog under her arm and sat down opposite the gentleman. As soon as the train started she leant across and told the smoker that he was no gentleman to smoke in the presence of a lady. Astounded, he pointed out that the compartment was labelled "smoking". Without hesitation she stood up, snatched the cigarette from his mouth and threw it out of the window.

"Ah, my beauty", he thought, "I'll pay you out for this directly". But how? Then an idea struck him: he would challenge her right to bring a dog into the compartment! So he did, and just as the train was nearing St. James's Park he seized the dog and dropped it out of the window. Precipitate action indeed, as the lady would now have him charged for killing her dog. When the train stopped, both passengers alighted, an inspector was called, and after the train had departed the tunnel mouth was examined with a lantern. And what did they see there? Yes, the dog, sitting between the tracks "as happy as a king", smoking the cigarette.[49] The lady in the case would have outraged MacCarthy O'Moore, author of *Tips for Travellers* (1899), who was shocked to find that there were "women who do not scruple to invade that *sanctum sanctorum*, the smoking compartment itself".[50]

Whatever the motive of the lady with the dog, she was surely not one of the "designing women who live by acting on the fears of railway passengers, and extorting money from them". Yet such women there were, and it was their presence that contributed to the growing demand, by male passengers, for the provision of "ladies only" compartments in the 1870s. The interests of "unprotected gentlemen" would be served, it was thought, by encouraging women travelling alone to travel together in their own accommodation.[51]

The Met responded, in 1874, with a very English compromise, by reserving on all its trains "compartments for ladies, and gentlemen accompanied by ladies", though policing the legitimacy of the male presence must have been a delicate task. The provision was later discontinued because the compartments were frequently empty, and when the trains were crowded there was a "natural angry grumbling of the passengers at the wasted space". Other railway companies that reserved compartments for ladies only also found that female passengers were reluctant to use them; nonetheless, their provision was widespread by the 1890s. In 1899 MacCarthy O'Moore still felt it necessary to warn men of the danger of entering compartments occupied by "strange women".[52]

---

48.   *IG* 4.10.1888
49.   *BST* 3.12.1892
50.   Quoted in Course p. 248
51.   *SLP* 3.10.1874
52.   Course p. 248, *ROG* March 1888

Where Are We Now?

Most compartment interiors, whether well-appointed first class, tolerable second class, or spartan third class, were unadorned with decoration, printed information, advertising or distractions of any kind. Passengers simply read their papers (if there was enough light), looked out of the window (in daylight), conversed with others (if they had to), or lost themselves in thought. A young lady travelling alone from Wandsworth Road (LCDR) to Winchmore Hill (GNR) in 1881, tiring of the many station stops, had fallen into a daydream. Suddenly she looked up "and saw the train gliding out of King's Cross and carrying me I knew not whither!" As she was in an MR train she should have changed to a GNR train at King's Cross. An on-train passenger information system would have saved her the inconvenience of an abortive journey to Camden Road and back.[53]

In the late Victorian era passengers relied mostly on the shouting of porters to remind them where they were and where they had to change. An exception, towards the end of the period, was the MDR, which in 1894 experimented with a "next station" indicator fitted in each compartment. The system was described as "simple, strong, and automatic, imposing no additional labour on either the guard or engine-driver". The indicator was activated when a lever beneath the carriage came in contact with a device placed at rail level, the station names being printed on cards arranged in consecutive order in a glass-fronted case mounted near the roof of the compartment. A bell rang as each card changed. "The adoption of such a scheme as this", said the *Railway Official Gazette*, "undoubtedly would prove a boon to passengers, who often vainly search for the name of the station among numberless advertisements on a not overbrilliantly illuminated platform". But woe betide the railway company if the system failed; it was predicted that passengers missing important engagements might sue the company for damages![54]

Almost two years later it was reported that only three MDR trains had been fitted with the system, and as the company ran nearly 400 carriages it would clearly be a long time before all trains were equipped.[55] Another two years passed before the system became widespread, but even then it was not in use on all branches of the MDR. Very few failures had been reported, but the equipment was expensive. It had been paid for partly by revenue raised from advertisements displayed, rather too prominently it was said, above the name of the next station. A contemporary engraving of a first class compartment shows that by this time (c.1897) advertisements were also displayed in frames beneath the luggage racks. The Met did not adopt the "next station" indicators, so Inner Circle passengers using that company's trains had to do without them.[56]

Another idea, suggested as early as 1874, was to display in each compartment a list of stations in sequence, up and down the line. It was claimed that in its absence travellers are "kept in a perpetual state of fidget as to arriving at their destination, and incessantly bother

53.   Hodge P, *The Cresswells of Winchmore Hill* (1999) p. 127
54.   *ROG* April 1894
55.   *ROG* Dec.1895
56.   Emmerson p. 69

the passengers and officials with questions, such as inquiring at Blackfriars whether that
is Brixton, or at Camberwell whether the Crystal Palace comes next".[57] One problem on
most suburban lines would have been how to ensure that the correct lists of stations were
displayed when carriages were redeployed from one line to another; there would also have
been the possibility of passengers being misled when trains were scheduled to omit certain
station stops.

In an attempt to brighten the interiors of all classes of carriage, the GER in 1888 began
displaying in its compartments photographs of places of interest and pleasure resorts served
by the company:

> *Many people, in travelling, do not care to read – they tire of gazing
> at the fast-fleeting landscape – and a series of well-arranged and
> artistically-executed photographs affords a break in the monotony.
> ...As a means of advertising, too, this novel introduction – especially
> on the suburban lines – is one which ought to bring the company in
> an increased revenue during the holiday season.*[58]

So the suburban traveller from Chingford or Chadwell Heath, staring longingly at the
pictures displayed in his compartment, might be tempted to holiday in Cromer or Great
Yarmouth – travelling there by GER of course. With this initiative the GER set an example
that other companies would follow; the compartment decorated with pictures of coast,
countryside and historic buildings reached by the line became one of the most enduring
images of rail travel in the late nineteenth and early twentieth centuries.

---

57. *SLP* 11.4.1874
58. *ROG* Dec.1888

Our Artist (*who has strolled into a London terminus*). "What's the matter with all these people? Is there a panic?"

Porter. "Panic! No, this ain't no panic. These is excursionists. Their train leaves in two hours, so they want to get a seat!"

CHAPTER 7

FELLOW PASSENGERS

Marks of Respectability

The varying standards of accommodation in first, second and third class carriages were matched if not exceeded in difference by the outward appearance and human characteristics of those who travelled in them. Here is a picture of third class passengers using a workmen's train on the Met in 1865:

> Early as was the hour, we found the platform all of a bustle with men, many of whom had bass baskets in their hands, or tin flagons, or basins done up in red handkerchiefs. Some few carried large saws under their arms, and beneath the overcoat of others one could just see a little bit of the flannel jacket worn by carpenters, whilst some were habited in the grey and clay-stained fustian peculiar to ground labourers.

The third class carriages were filled with plasterers, joiners and labourers as the train progressed from Bishop's Road to Farringdon Street. Here was a butcher on his way to Smithfield Market, a newsvendor going to fetch his morning papers, a carpenter in a grey slouch hat – "one of those strange growling and grumbling passengers so often met with among the working classes".[1]

Different indeed was the crowd making its way into London Bridge Station on Derby Day, 1874, for the LBSCR special trains to Epsom Downs:

> The majority arrived on foot, and their external attire was very similar, negligé hats of straw or white felt, light or lightish coats ornamented with the indispensable race-glass. ...The special fare was eight shillings return, so that ensured a certain degree of respectability.

Less respectable was the unseemly rush for the first class carriages, of which there were only a few on each train, the special fare applying to all classes:

1.　　Walford pp. 232–233 quoting a brochure of 1865

> *What ladies there were, literally pulled themselves together, regardless of*
> *appearances, and bolted. The younger men forged ahead, and pushed and*
> *passed the weaker ones... the old, the awkward, the laden, and the free all*
> *came rushing on as if pursued by the mad dog.*

"It seems odd", concluded the writer, "that a number of apparently English gentlemen should first of all imperil their lives by clutching at a passing train, and then engage in something very like a free fight for the possession of a cushioned seat during a short pleasure journey".[2]

Third class growling and first class greed – tempered, one might assume, by second class respectability. Not so, according to a columnist in the *Holloway Press*, commenting in 1891 on the partial abolition of second class accommodation on the GNR:

> *Society would not lose much if the railway companies could as easily*
> *abolish the class of people who usually travel "second". I think that these*
> *people, as a rule, may be taken to be the most unsociable, uncomfortable,*
> *grumbling, disagreeable people in creation.*

The writer regretted that the abolition of second class applied initially to main line traffic only: "I am very sorry that the Great Northern Railway deem it necessary to pander to the vanity of such folks on our local line".[3]

Friction could occur when passengers were obliged to share accommodation with those of a different social class. The railway companies' attempts to separate workmen and other travellers were not always successful. Third class carriages were not the sole preserve of workmen, and complaints were sometimes made against their dirty clothes and bad language by other third class passengers. The general manager of the GER was acutely aware of this when, in 1884, he gave evidence to the Royal Commission on the Housing of the Working Classes. Suburban trains leaving Liverpool Street between 5 and 6 p.m., he said, were

> *...filled with well-to-do City men and their wives and daughters; and it*
> *is not an agreeable thing for them to hobnob with these working men,*
> *excellent men perhaps in their walk of life, but the language which they*
> *naturally use is very offensive to most people.*

Dirty clothes and bad language were not all. The workmen spat, smoked evil-smelling pipes, cut off the leather window straps in the carriages, and even cooked herrings on the waiting room fires.[4]

Occasionally a first class passenger would be incommoded by the pretensions of a social inferior. A washerwoman who travelled regularly on the Crystal Palace line of the

2.   *RFS* June 1874
3.   *Holloway & Hornsey Press* 30.10.1891
4.   Kellett pp. 97–98

LCDR decided that she would buy a first class season ticket, at a time when these tickets were "reasonable in price". When she entered a first class compartment one day laden with a basket of linen, a director of the Crystal Palace Company seated in the same compartment was so outraged that he was "determined to put a stop to such a state of things". The result, it was claimed, was an increase in the price of season tickets to the palace.[5]

How different was the attitude of another first class passenger on the Crystal Palace line in 1890! A large crowd trying to board a heavily loaded train noticed a first class compartment occupied by only two people – a lady and gentleman – with a "reserved" label on the window. About a dozen people made for the door, but the guard prevented them from entering. The gentleman, coming to the window, said "never mind, let them in". "Can't, sir", said the guard, "the compartment is reserved". The gentleman insisted that, as he had reserved it, the passengers should be allowed in. "All right", said the guard, "but as I may get into trouble, please give me your card". "That is unnecessary", came the reply, "I am the Marquis of Lorne". The lady was the Princess Louise.[6]

Out-of-class travel was sometimes unavoidable, especially in crowded conditions. On the underground railway it was complained that:

> *People are compelled to plunge into what carriages they find opposite*
> *them, and as the companies do not hesitate to crowd any class of carriage*
> *with any class of passenger when the exigencies of the line require it...*
> *what right have they to complain if passengers follow their example, and*
> *do the best they can for themselves?*

It was considered absurd for the underground railway companies to impose penalties for travelling in a higher class of carriage than the ticket held "where trains only stop an instant, and all is hurry-scurry, struggle, scuffle, and confusion". And if the companies did insist on fining such passengers, should they not compensate those who were forced to travel in a lower class of carriage than they had paid for?[7]

Some of the miseries of third class travel were unwillingly endured by a first class passenger from London Bridge Station on Christmas Eve, 1891. He arrives to find the station

> *...cold, slippery, foggy and miserable. Crowds of holiday makers*
> *attempting to be jolly under many difficulties. Fog getting into the lungs*
> *of everyone. Fidgety passengers grumbling, officials hoarsely shouting,*
> *engines whistling, and apparently chaos.*

The train is late, the first class is full, and the carriages are so crowded that this first class passenger is advised by a porter to travel third class, standing. The journey to Croydon is made with a "grumpy lot of curmudgeons":

5.   *SLP* 19.2.1881
6.   *ROG* Aug.1890 quoting *Court Journal*
7.   *SLP* 14.9.1872

LOGIC

Stout Party. " What ! no room !   Ain't that man just got
out ?   If people can get out, people can get in ! "

A BANK HOLIDAY SKETCH

Facetious Individual (from carriage window). " Change 'ere,
'ave we ?   Then kindly oblige me with a sardine-opener ! "

Miserable-looking man with red nose grumbles at lateness in starting.
Miserable man's wife with redder nose grumbles at people having cheek
to stand. Train runs slowly along for a mile or two then stops. Miserable
man takes advantage to state he thinks we are now on spot where terrible
accident occurred. Fog signal. Red-nosed woman screams.

Eventually the train runs into a dim and foggy station, which someone suggests is East Croydon. The first class passenger alights, wishing he had not taken the porter's advice.[8]

Standing Room Only

Victorian railway travellers did not expect to have to stand, even on short suburban journeys. Long trains of compartment carriages seating ten or twelve per compartment maximised the number of seats available. The purchase of a railway ticket was considered by passengers to carry with it the entitlement to a seat.

The reality was very different, especially on the busy metropolitan lines. "It is not uncommon, on wet days", said a user of the LCDR Metropolitan Extension in 1872, "to see first, second, and third-class carriages choked up with people standing as thick as sardines in a box". Whatever the weather, it was quite normal on this line to find third class 12-seat compartments with six additional passengers standing between the seats, and one user reported no fewer than thirteen standing passengers in a 12-seat compartment. Moreover, the compartments marked for twelve seats could, it was claimed, seat only ten in comfort. Second class season ticket holders on the same line complained if their 10-seat compartments carried five standing passengers, but they felt entitled to more space for the extra fare. The overcrowding was aggravated by "station staff habitually inviting passengers to enter compartments which are already over-full".[9]

Similar problems occurred north of the river. Complaints of overcrowding in third class carriages on the NLR were voiced in 1882. A correspondent from Dalston was unhappy that the practice of allowing passengers to ride in the brakevans of heavily loaded trains had been stopped. Another from the same area said that he was obliged to travel second class and pay an excess fare as the third class was so crowded.[10]

In 1883 the *Spectator* attacked the railway companies for the appalling level of overcrowding in third class carriages:

...the crowd pushes and almost fights, the compartments are sweltering
pens, and the overcrowding is positively dangerous. The people will not
be left behind, and submit to anything rather than lose a train. ...The
passengers are at such times packed like goods, while paying eight times

---

8.   *ROG* Jan.1892
9.   *SLP* 13.1.1872, 20.1.1872, 19.2.1881, 3.2.1883, 13.10.1883, 15.2.1890
10. *Hackney & Kingsland Gazette* 17.5.1882, 29.11.1882

as much; and the companies declare that it is their own fault, or the fault
of circumstances, and that there is no remedy.

The writer felt that only the Board of Trade could act to improve the situation by imposing fines on the companies, and that this would encourage them to deal with the problem by redesigning carriages and controlling the numbers boarding them:

Overcrowding should be prohibited absolutely and finally, and
supplementary trains run where needful, at a small increase of fare, as a
fitting penalty for being too late. In short, it should be as easy for anybody,
however feeble, to enter a third-class compartment in the morning or
evening as it is to enter a sixpenny omnibus. [11]

The problem did not go away, and on some lines it worsened towards the end of the century. By the early 1890s growth in the GNR's suburban traffic was proving an embarrassment to the company. A regular passenger from King's Cross to Palmers Green claimed that it was not unusual to find up to twenty-eight passengers in a compartment (i.e. sixteen standing) and to have to stand for the whole journey.[12] By 1897 the *Hornsey and Finsbury Park Journal* had accepted that the GNR could neither lengthen its suburban trains nor run more and that the only solution was to build a new line.[13] In the following year a Bounds Green resident forwarded to the GNR a "memorial" signed by 233 season ticket holders – including county magistrates, county and district councillors, and members of the Stock Exchange – objecting to the worsening overcrowding, but the company entered the new century with the issue unresolved.[14]

The GER faced similar problems towards the end of the century. Despite its novel decision to widen carriages to seat twelve instead of ten per compartment, overcrowding continued to worsen. A daily passenger from Enfield to Liverpool Street protested in 1901 that "invariably the third-class carriages are packed like proverbial herrings in a barrel, ten or twelve standing down the centre of each compartment". As with the GNR, the local press seemed to be resigned to the fact that the GER simply could not run any more trains, in this case because of the bottleneck at Bishopsgate.[15]

A recurring issue on London's railways throughout the late nineteenth century was the right of passengers seated in a train to prevent further passengers from entering a compartment when all the seats were taken. Passengers who were prepared to stand had, in effect, to obtain permission to do so from the seated passengers. If one seated passenger objected, no passenger could insist on standing.

The right of seated passengers to act in this way was upheld in the courts several times

11.   Quoted in *ROG* Aug.1883
12.   *Palmers Green & Southgate Gazette* 23.5.1930
13.   *HFPJ* 11.9.1897
14.   *North Middlesex Chronicle* 31.12.1898
15.   *Tottenham & Edmonton Weekly Herald* 5.4.1901

during the late nineteenth century, but had it been widely exercised or enforced, hundreds of passengers would have been left behind. Normally common sense prevailed, most seated passengers being well aware that on some other occasion they might themselves wish to stand to avoid delay. Now and again, however, the right was insisted upon, and friction between passengers, with or without the involvement of railway staff, sometimes ensued.

In August 1883 a foreman porter employed at Camden Road Station (MR) appeared at Marylebone Police Court to answer a summons for assaulting a passenger travelling from Moorgate Street to Crouch Hill. Before the train left Moorgate Street the compartment in which the complainant was travelling became full with its complement of ten seated passengers, and the complainant turned the lock on the door to prevent any more passengers from entering. At Camden Road another passenger wished to enter the compartment; initially the occupants prevented it, but the defendant and other porters managed to open the door to allow the intending passenger to get in: "a scene of the greatest confusion ensued. The passengers' hats were knocked off, and the defendant caught hold of the complainant by the throat, and, holding up his fist, threatened what he would do to him if he were only in the 'open' ". The episode was ended by the intervention of the stationmaster. The magistrate confirmed the complainant's right to prevent entry to the compartment, and "was very glad to see someone public-spirited enough to take up the cudgels on behalf of the travelling public, for the gentlemen in question were strictly within their rights in acting as they did". The porter was fined five shillings plus one guinea costs.[16]

In a comparable incident at King's Cross five years later, the confrontation was between seated and standing passengers without the involvement of railway staff. In mid-January 1888 train services in all parts of London had been affected by dense fog, causing much overcrowding. When a train pulled in to King's Cross, a party of five "sporting characters" on the platform attempted to enter a first class compartment in which all seats were taken. One of them tried to move the door handle, but an occupant of the compartment held it firmly and "sarcastically grinned" at the frantic but vain attempts of the intending passengers to gain entry.

Events then took an unexpected turn. Instead of trying another door, the party retired to a seat at the back of the platform, apparently to await the next train. But as the first train was slowly moving out of the platform they suddenly made a rush for the door of the compartment they had tried to enter, and one of them seized the handle: "A smart twist, the door flew open, and the party, giving vent to a wild yell, forced themselves bodily inside. The comfortably-seated occupants were greatly astonished, whilst the intruders chuckled freely". Given the serious disruption to the train service, a passenger who witnessed this incident had no sympathy for the seated first class passengers: "the avaricious specimens of humanity who fix the carriage door, at times when the traffic is deranged by uncontrollable causes, must be classed as nothing short of contemptuous wretches".[17]

One more confrontation of this kind, occurring at Waterloo Station later in 1888, must be recorded here if only for the deft but shameless manner in which the dispute was handled.

---

16. *North Middlesex Chronicle* 1.9.1883
17. *IG* 16.1.1888

A gentleman entered a full compartment on an Epsom train with the request "will you kindly allow me to stand?" "Certainly not, sir!" exclaimed a passenger in a corner seat. "As you appear to be the only person who objects to my presence", came the reply, "I shall remain where I am". At this the protesting passenger rose from his seat, put his head out of the window, and summoned the guard; meanwhile the newcomer quietly slipped into the vacant seat. The guard arrived and asked what the trouble was. "One over the number", replied the newcomer, coolly. As the train was about to leave, the guard pulled the protesting passenger out of the compartment, leaving him gesticulating wildly on the platform.[18]

A Variety of Nuisances

Late Victorian rail travellers, trapped within the confines of a compartment for the duration of their journey, could not escape the activities of their fellow passengers. These were at times unwelcome, and occasionally unpleasant or even dangerous.

Itinerant preachers, singers and instrumentalists, drunken youths, hooligans, bearers of evil-smelling baggage, and even "ladies of easy virtue", contributed their own particular brands of nuisance to disturb or distress the innocent passenger. Third class passengers in carriages without full-height partitions between the compartments were especially vulnerable to some of these nuisances.

In 1881 a third class passenger on the LCDR between Peckham Queen's Road and Loughborough Junction complained of the "preaching annoyance" on a Sunday train. The preacher had an audience of about eighteen passengers in the carriage; he was asked to desist or leave the train, but his speech became more violent and he tried to distribute handbills. He grossly insulted one gentleman, saying that he was "leading a life of infamy". A brawl ensued, and the guard was called to intervene at the next station.[19] In 1894 an early morning passenger travelling third class on the GER from Seven Sisters to Liverpool Street complained about a party of "fanatics" who passed the journey in singing, praying and preaching, causing a nuisance to other passengers and turning the carriage into "a travelling mission hall".[20]

"When are the authorities of the North London Railway going to stop the banjo and fiddle nuisance on their line?" asked a columnist in 1888. Parties of musicians had been playing on the line for years, changing carriages at nearly every station and begging for money. "As nervous people do not like to refuse... they are in a sense blackmailed by these importunate people." The nuisance would not be tolerated on an omnibus or tramcar, so "perhaps the directors of the line will take the hint, and give us one reason less for preferring tramways to a North London train".[21]

They evidently did not do so, for six years later the editor of the *Kilburn Times* complained:

---

18.   *ROG* Aug.1888 quoting *London Railway Review*
19.   *SLP* 4.6.1881
20.   Lake G, *The Railways of Tottenham* (1945) p. 61
21.   *IG* 18.10.1888

> *There is a youth who affects the North London Line with a dulcimer,*
> *whom we never meet without experiencing an overwhelming desire to*
> *slay him. We have known him now for six years, and several strings of his*
> *instrument have been getting looser and more twangy every day during*
> *that time.*

The only hope, it seemed, was that the instrument would eventually break down altogether, and that the owner would never be able to raise the funds to buy another. But that would not put an end to the other "wandering fiddlers, concertina performers, zither players, and tin whistlers, who torture one from station to station, and then thrust greasy caps between your eyes and your paper for backsheesh".[22]

Assaults on trains by drunken passengers – usually young men – were reported to be on the increase in the 1880s. Early in 1883 a gentleman, "well-known" in south London, suffered an unnerving experience in a first class compartment at Peckham Rye. The incident started at Ludgate Hill, when a tall, athletic young man, who appeared to be "half-intoxicated", entered the compartment and argued his claim for the gentleman's corner seat (although the other corner seats were unoccupied). Failing to unseat the gentleman, he then entered a neighbouring compartment, but at every station alighted onto the platform and shook his fist at the gentleman through the window. On arrival at Peckham Rye, the ruffian entered the gentleman's compartment and assaulted the defenceless passenger, pulling him to the ground. Police were called, but railway officials failed to detain the train until an arrest had been made, and the perpetrator was able to escape by getting back into the train.[23]

We have noted the cutting off of leather window straps on GER workmen's trains, but other reports of passengers causing wanton damage to trains are rare. However, a further example comes from the GER. Around the turn of the century the company introduced new second class carriages – "nicely upholstered, and altogether as comfortable as need be". Above the seats on both sides of each compartment were notices reading "to seat six". In 1901 it was observed that in many of the compartments part of the lettering had been scratched out – presumably the first letter of "seat". "If we had our way", said the *Tottenham and Edmonton Weekly Herald*, "we would compel these ignoramuses to travel in cattle trucks, in which, undoubtedly, they would feel more at home".[24]

The poor personal hygiene of some passengers would have been all too evident in the close atmosphere of a railway compartment, but certain unwelcome odours were more occupational than personal. One such was the smell of dirty washing, experienced by a traveller on the Met between the City and Hammersmith on a Monday afternoon in 1871·

> *...there appeared on the platform of the Portland Road Station several*
> *buxom laundresses, bound, as I heard, for the Latimer Road. As soon as*
> *our train arrives they bundle themselves into our compartment with their*

22.   *Kilburn Times* 24.8.1894
23.   *SLP* 20.1.1883
24.   *Tottenham & Edmonton Weekly Herald* 18.1.1901

baskets of foul linen, at which I must confess to the weakness of being a
little disgusted.

On suggesting to a porter who assisted them that the guard's van was the proper place for these huge bundles of dirty clothes, the passenger received the following reply: "Ah sir, our guards has got very particular what they haves in their van since this 'ere small pox has been about, dirty clothes 'specially, so they won't have 'em".[25] Other smells, though unpleasant, were less hazardous to health. A GNR traveller from New Southgate in the 1880s recalled the lingering stink of fish in the carriages after they had been occupied by fishmongers travelling home from Billingsgate in the early hours with their laden baskets.[26]

The on-train activities of "ladies of easy virtue" were rarely if ever recorded. But public concern was expressed at the nuisance caused by "disorderly women" congregating at Richmond Station on summer evenings. Their proceedings in the vicinity of the station were, it was alleged, "especially abominable" and "of the most disgusting description". They would shout "the most filthy expressions" so loudly that residents near the station had to close their windows. By 1889 the nuisance had become so pronounced that magistrates were urged to "exhibit a greater determination to put down the evil. The usual fine is easily paid out of the wages of sin; what is needed is a sentence of imprisonment"; and it was suggested that the churches should lead a movement against "this moral canker in our midst".[27]

---

25. *West London Observer* 1.7.1871
26. *Palmers Green & Southgate Gazette* 23.5.1930
27. *RTT* 4.5.1889, 29.6.1889

CHAPTER 8

HAZARDS OF THE JOURNEY

Late Again!

Poor punctuality was a major source of dissatisfaction among late Victorian rail travellers in London, and some companies acquired unenviable reputations for not running their trains on time. The East London Railway, opened in 1869 through Marc Brunel's Thames Tunnel, ran no trains itself, so it was easy to deflect blame for bad timekeeping onto the companies providing the train service. The LBSCR trains that used the East London Railway were said to be "proverbially late – so late, that it seemed as if they at times had been lost in the dark".[1]

The blame game was played by many railway companies that exercised running powers over other companies' lines or accommodated other companies' trains on their own tracks. In presenting his half-yearly report to shareholders in January 1874, the chairman of the Met claimed that delays occurred "through our being impeded by the trains of other companies" – of which there were 416 out of a total of 960 trains operated daily over the Met's own lines. However, this had to be seen against the background of a generally good punctuality record.[2]

Less commendable was the performance of the LCDR's Metropolitan Extension Line, on which trains were alleged to be "always late". But there was some understanding by travellers of the difficulties of keeping time on this busy stretch of railway. One of the speakers at a public meeting of LCDR passengers at Peckham in July 1877 blamed poor punctuality on the running of trains of four different companies – LCDR, GNR, MR and LSWR – over the same route, and their dependence on "the clearance of the congested traffic on the Metropolitan Underground Railway". He thought that when the proposed connection to the SER was opened (the Union Street Spur of 1878) the situation would get even worse and the result would be "a chaos" (at which point a voice from the floor shouted, "a total smash to a certainty").[3]

In November 1889 an LSWR passenger wrote to his local newspaper about frequent delays on his daily journeys between Richmond and Waterloo. In one week – "a week clear from fogs and one which, I can assure you, is a very fair average week" – he suffered total delays

1. *SLP* 21.7.1883
2. *RFS* Feb.1874
3. *Camberwell News* 28.7.1877

REGULAR IRREGULARITY

Passenger (in a hurry). " Is this train punctual? "
Porter. " Yessir, generally a quarter of an hour late to
a minute! "

of ninety-one minutes – "or, say, at the rate of over seventy-eight hours per annum wasted". His complaint was supported by the paper's editor, who argued that railway companies should not be able to escape liability for the consequences of late-running trains.[4] The correspondence brought forth a volley of complaints about LSWR punctuality in the ensuing weeks.

Another source of delay to passengers on the LSWR was the practice of cancelling regular trains to accommodate special trains to race meetings, especially Ascot. "There is no knowing what the South-Western Railway Company may not do to meet the convenience of their race patrons", screamed a columnist in June 1889. "The interests of regular customers are sent to the winds when these occasional patrons require consideration." A colleague on the same newspaper indulged in sarcasm at the LSWR's expense when he claimed to be:

---

4.   *RTT* 30.11.1889

...fully alive to the necessity which arises during any of the... race meetings of suspending the greater part of the usual train service, and putting the general public to a considerable amount of inconvenience.[5]

The problem remained. Ten years later, a newspaper correspondent hoping to travel from Richmond to Waterloo on an Ascot race day found that his train had been taken off and none of the officials could tell him when there would be another. Instead he travelled to town on the MDR, and successfully claimed a refund on his ticket to Waterloo.[6]

A similar difficulty faced LSWR passengers between Brentford and Barnes on boat race days. For many years it was the practice to stand trains on Barnes Bridge during the boat race and charge spectators a high price to use the trains as a grandstand. "This is all very well for the company and the fortunate occupants of the trains, but there are doubtless many people who cannot waste time upon boat races, and yet if they have occasion to use the line in question on the day... they are seriously incommoded by the disjointure of the traffic which must occur."[7]

Delays resulting from missed connections were very irritating for some passengers. In June 1889 an LCDR passenger from Peckham Rye to Ludgate Hill was advised to change at Brixton rather than wait for a through train. After some delay the train from Peckham arrived at Brixton, and as the passengers were crossing the footbridge to the up platform the guard of the Ludgate Hill train standing there whistled it away – appearing "to take quite a delight in the act". That gave the passengers twenty-five minutes "in which to admire the manifold beauties of the Brixton Station". They finally arrived at Ludgate Hill one hour after leaving Peckham, "and some minute or two longer time than the express takes to go from London Bridge to Brighton!"[8]

A north Londoner experienced delay of a similar kind on several journeys from Kilburn (LNWR) to an unspecified NLR station beyond Camden Town in 1894. He had to change from an LNWR train to an NLR train at Chalk Farm, and although there was evidently a planned connection it was often missed, adding about fifteen minutes to the journey:

If [the train] *left before I got there I shouldn't mind the quarter of an hour's wait, enlivened as it has been this week on two occasions with a capital view of a porter's football match with bundles of evening newspapers – excellent use to put them to – but when I see the train apparently waiting for me, when it allows me to get as far as the top of the steps leading to the platform whence it departs, and then goes off with a little defiant shriek, I am tempted to become profane.*

5.   *RTT* 15.6.1889, 22.6.1889
6.   *RTT* 26.8.1899
7.   *RTT* 22.4.1899
8.   *SLP* 15.6.1889

"It does seem curious to my small un-railwaylike mind", concludes the writer, "that these trains, supposed to run in conjunction with one another, should exhibit such perversities".[9]

Occasionally an incident on the line would cause delays of spectacular proportions. On Whit Monday 1875, when 94,000 people visited the Alexandra Palace, mostly by the GNR, "the railway service was quite unequal to the occasion". Big trouble started early in the evening, when crowds were beginning to return from the palace. A collision between an engine and a coal train in Copenhagen Tunnel, between Holloway and King's Cross, blocked both lines. Heavily loaded trains were soon backed up all the way from Holloway to Alexandra Palace. Excursionists endured the delay patiently for an hour or two, after which those nearest to the London end of the blockage climbed down from the trains (eventually under the direction of railway officials) and "stampeded" along the line:

Fathers and mothers carrying sleeping children, groups of girls with their sweethearts, noisy youths and men, many of them the worse for drink, swarmed down the line, forming a scene of indescribable confusion and excitement.

PASSENGERS WAITING FOR THE TRAIN IN THE
FLOODED DISTRICTS

9.   *Kilburn Times* 23.11.1894

It was past midnight when they poured out onto the Caledonian Road, with no means of getting home. Many walked to King's Cross to seek refreshment, and the crowd did not disperse until after 2 a.m. Massive delays occurred to long distance train services from King's Cross; the Scotch Mail started nine hours late. The blockage was not cleared until eight o'clock the following morning.[10]

The rapid growth of suburban traffic on the GNR caused major congestion and delay on the approaches to King's Cross from the mid-1870s. Early in 1876 the four-mile journey from Farringdon Street to Finsbury Park was reported to be taking up to three quarters of an hour.[11] Similar delays occurred frequently throughout the 1880s and into the 1890s. By 1891 users of the High Barnet branch had become so desperate that they were planning to promote a wholly new railway line, connecting with the LNWR at Gospel Oak, "else the present prosperity and growth of the neighbourhood is likely to receive a severe check".[12]

The MR too had its bottleneck – at Kentish Town. Although the volume of suburban traffic was only a fraction of that carried on the GNR, serious delays occurred during the 1880s at the junction with the South Tottenham line, where suburban trains were held to give priority to late-running expresses to St. Pancras.[13] Further delays on the South Tottenham line were caused by the not infrequent flooding of Crouch Hill Station after heavy rain. In August 1888 a severe thunderstorm flooded the station to a depth of six feet, causing all traffic to be suspended after 11.30 p.m. The last train to South Tottenham was detained at Hornsey Road Station at 12.10 a.m., and passengers had to remain in it until 4.30 a.m. – "a novel experience" said the local newspaper. The problem continued into the 1890s; in July 1897 the station was flooded to a depth of seven feet, the worst then recorded.[14]

When delays occurred, it was often the lack of information to passengers that attracted most criticism. An engine failure on the MDR at Charing Cross in January 1886 caused extensive delay to an estimated 3,000 to 4,000 passengers stranded on eight trains. Among them was the Common Serjeant, who was late in taking his seat at the Central Criminal Court; a juryman pointedly remarked that when he had been delayed by a late train he had been fined for non-attendance – a remark, commented the press, that deserved the attention of the railway companies:

> *The railway officials might take the hint thrown out, and afford some information to passengers as to the cause of delay or the probable duration of the stoppage, in order that they might leave the train and proceed to their destinations by another route.*[15]

In January 1893 GNR passengers from Moorgate Street were stranded owing to a lack of effective communication between the Met and the GNR. Two derailed wagons between

10. *Tottenham & Edmonton Weekly Herald* 22.5.1875
11. *North Metropolitan & Holloway Press* 15.1.1876
12. *Tottenham & Edmonton Weekly Herald* 7.8.1891
13. Sekon p. 189
14. *IG* 3.8.1888, *HFPJ* 24.7.1897
15. *West London Observer* 16.1.1886

Farringdon Street and King's Cross had blocked the line late one evening. Passengers waiting for a GNR train to High Barnet were advised to travel by the Met from Moorgate Street, Aldersgate Street and Farringdon Street to King's Cross, where, they were assured, a GNR train from the terminus would be held back to accommodate them. On arrival at King's Cross terminus, however, the passengers found to their dismay that the last High Barnet train had gone. Eventually an inspector was found, but he claimed to have no knowledge of the arrangements, and when asked to organise transport for the stranded passengers replied: "I can't do that; you may have the waiting-room, or get home the best way you can". Most took cabs in preference to a cold night on a waiting room bench.[16]

When trains did run to time the public took it for granted and rarely voiced their appreciation. It was left to the railway companies to claim the credit, and this they often did at half-yearly meetings. In March 1889, for example, the chairman of the NLR attributed the company's financial success to "careful management, the efficiency of the line and works, and to paying the greatest attention to the punctuality of the trains" – even at the expense of missed connections, perhaps! In the same month the chairman of the MDR positively smarted at the lack of public recognition of the company's good performance, pointing out

> ...the great advantages offered by the railway in times of fog, snow, and rain. On such occasions the cabman puts up his fare when he can get along, the omnibuses put up their fares, the steamers do not work at all. ...Why do we not put up our fares on these occasions? ...The public are sadly ungrateful.[17]

The idea of raising railway fares during inclement weather was certainly a novel one!

Passengers at Risk

Carelessness or even recklessness by passengers sometimes resulted in delay, injury, or occasionally death. Among accidents caused or contributed to by passengers, the greatest number arose from travellers joining or alighting from moving trains. The problem was acute on the underground lines, where short stopping times and large crowds encouraged passengers to enter or leave trains in motion and risk falling from footboards or being struck by swinging doors.[18] An example of the sort of incident that could occur was reported by a correspondent to the *Globe* in 1872:

> At South Kensington, just as the train was about to start, a well-dressed young lady ran to the first-class carriage in which my wife and I were, pushed violently one of the porters who tried to hold her back,

---

16.   *East London Advertiser* 28.1.1893
17.   *ROG* March 1889
18.   *RSOG* Jan.1877

*and flung herself in. She fell on her face on the floor of the carriage,
whilst the whole of the lower part of the body was hanging outside the
open door with the train in motion. With great exertions my wife and
I succeeded in dragging her into the carriage, when we were coolly
told that if people would but have left her alone, she could have done
it well enough.* [19]

The practice of fining passengers on the underground railway who displayed such
recklessness was widely condemned, if only because railway officials encouraged it by
despatching trains prematurely, and railway guards set a bad example by waiting until their
train had gathered speed before jumping from the platform into their van. The experience
of "a little dapper elderly looking man" waiting for a train at Edgware Road in 1873 should
have served as a lesson to all. Having watched the "right away" being given to an Addison
Road train, he observed that the guard "waited until the last compartment reached him, and
then raising one hand to the rail, and lifting one foot lightly from the platform, he swung
majestically around, screwed himself like a billiard ball into his narrow compartment, and
the next moment was hid from sight in the tunnel".

Our dapper friend was deeply impressed by the guard's apparently effortless acrobatics,
and his eyes glistened with anticipation at the arrival of the next train. He waited until the
green flag had been waved and the train was gathering speed:

*Then raising his hand and leg just as he had seen the guard do, and
looking carelessly away, just as the guard did, he reached out for the
rail of the last carriage, clutched a handful of steam, space and sulphur,
and the next instant was trying to push his head through the planks of the
platform, fighting the air with his heels, madly pawing around with his
hands, and using profane language at a fearful rate.*

Station staff pulled him to his feet and applied ice from the refreshment bar to his
head; he showed his gratitude by threatening legal action against the Metropolitan Railway
Company! [20]

A common cause or contributory factor in many accidents to passengers alighting from
trains was the gap between carriage footboard and platform. In 1878 Sir Francis Goldsmid,
formerly MP for Reading, fell from a train as it was arriving at Waterloo, caught his legs
between the carriage and platform, and sustained fatal injuries. Although the carriage door
may have been flung open, for whatever reason, before the train had stopped, the inquest
jury considered that the perpendicular distance from carriage to platform of up to thirty-one
inches, and the wide horizontal gap between footboard and platform, were contributory
causes of the accident. [21]

19.   Quoted in *SLP* 14.9.1872
20.   *RFS* Jan.1874
21.   *East London Observer* 11.5.1878

A similar issue arose with the extension of Met and MDR trains over the LSWR to Kew and Richmond in 1877. Whereas the carriage footboards were almost level with the platforms on the Inner Circle, they were two feet or more above the LSWR platforms. "Descent and ascent", it was observed, "in the cases of ladies particularly, were matters of arduous and perilous climbing".[22] On Thursday 5th July 1877 an accident to a passenger alighting from an MDR train at Richmond led to a court action which focused attention on the problem of varying platform heights. It was also an occasion for some hilarity, enjoyed at the expense of the railway companies involved.

On the day in question, a Petersham resident travelled by MDR train from Richmond to Temple, returning late the same evening, also on an MDR train. He arrived back at Richmond in the dark, missed the footboard on alighting, and fell forward onto the platform. His injuries incapacitated him for some time, causing loss of profits to his business. A few days after the accident he took his complaint to the stationmaster at Richmond (LSWR), who referred him to the MDR. The MDR referred him to the general manager of the LSWR, who referred him back to the MDR. That company declined his claim for compensation, on the grounds that he had bought his ticket from the LSWR.

Legal action followed against the MDR. As part of its defence the company argued that the plaintiff should have noticed when he boarded his outward train in daylight that there was a large gap between the carriage and the platform! "We have no power to alter the South-Western platform", argued Counsel for the MDR, to which the judge replied "but you could alter your carriage". The court found the MDR liable. "If the District Railway Company put their carriage upon a line which was not suited to it", said the judge, "they must take the responsibility of that act". The plaintiff was awarded £500 damages.[23]

Humorists made the most of the comic absurdity of the case. The magazine *Funny Folks* carried four cartoons illustrating how railway companies might assist passengers wishing to board or alight from carriages whose footboards were well above platform height. In the first, a portly gentleman gazes up in despair at the door of a railway carriage, the floor of which is well above his head. In the second cartoon, the gentleman is heaved into the carriage on the back of a porter, assisted by a passenger in the compartment. In the third picture, the passenger has arrived at his destination and a porter approaches with a blanket over his arm. The fourth scene shows two porters holding out the blanket while the luckless passenger dives into it head first from the train![24]

Punch addressed with characteristic humour the respective liability of the two railway companies involved, best settled "by an amicable arrangement concluded upon in a little quiet chat between railway chairmen". The two imaginary chairmen (Hobson and Jobson) consider first whether the passenger might have been at fault:

---

22.   *East London Observer* 11.5.1878
23.   Foulkes v. Metropolitan District Railway; *RTT* 25.1.1879
24.   *RTT* 8.2.1879, *Funny Folks* 8.2.1879

Hobson: *No, Jobby, there's no denying it, the fault was ours. Our train was one of which the carriages were no less than two feet above the level of the platform – by the way, your platform.*

Jobson: *Our platform is fully two feet below the level of your carriages. That is as much our fault as yours. Let us pay half.*

Hobson: *We will immediately level our carriages to your platforms.*

Jobson: *We, at the same time, will meet you half-way. We will elevate our platforms towards your carriages wherever we can.*

The chat concludes with an agreement to double the compensation:

Jobson: *Partners in negligence, Hobby, my boy. We will be sharers in its cost, and unite in setting an example to all Directors who meanly and ungenerously dispute their just liabilities in a Court of Law.* [25]

Comedy turned to tragedy when in 1879 two further accidents occurred to passengers alighting from MDR trains at Richmond, one of them resulting in a fatality. A Board of Trade inquiry concluded that the MDR carriages "were not fit carriages to be run to a platform of this kind". They had a continuous footboard projecting only two inches from the side of the carriage; this did not really act as a footboard at all, and at a low platform an alighting passenger could easily lose his footing. However, the Board of Trade had no power to require the platforms or carriages to be altered. [26]

Whatever their shortcomings as fitted to MDR trains, however, continuous footboards were widely welcomed for preventing falls between carriages and platforms. During 1878 the Board of Trade asked railway companies to state their views and intentions regarding the adoption of continuous footboards on their carriages. Most companies had replied by the beginning of 1879 (the LSWR being a notable exception), but carriages with short footboards terminating either side of the doors continued in use on some lines. [27] On Monday 29th March 1880, a passenger alighting from an NLR train at Camden Town fell between the carriage and the platform, was run over by the departing train, and died of his injuries. The coroner's inquest heard conflicting evidence as to whether or not the train was in motion when the victim alighted, but the verdict stated that "if continuous footboards had been attached to the train the accident would not have happened". [28]

An altogether different kind of accident arising from passenger action took place at Hampstead Heath Station (LNWR) on Easter Monday, 17th April 1892. The station handled

25. *Punch* 8.3.1879; the conversation is abbreviated here, but its essence is preserved.
26. *RTT* 12.7.1879
27. *RTT* 1.3.1879
28. *Times* 5.4.1880, 12.4.1880, 29.4.1880

large crowds on Bank Holidays, and an adverse change in the weather during the day could cause an unexpected rush of homeward-bound passengers. A sudden thunderstorm on that Easter Monday brought an uncontrollable crowd to the station, and in the resulting crush on the stairs down to the eastbound platform eight people lost their lives. Special arrangements were subsequently made to handle the traffic more safely, including the provision of a new footpath access to the station, and a few years later these were reported to be working well.[29]

Off the Rails

The chances of being involved in a train accident on London's late Victorian railways were small, but if a derailment or collision did occur, passengers travelling in relatively fragile, wooden-bodied carriages were vulnerable. This is not the place for a catalogue of railway accidents in London, nor for a detailed explanation of their technical and operational aspects, but a few examples described in outline will illustrate a variety of causes and consequences. Of the half-dozen train accidents to be mentioned, the first two were caused by signalling error, the second two by driver error, and the last two by equipment failure.

At Stepney (GER) on Bank Holiday Monday 5th August 1878 it was last-minute intervention by a signalman, rather than his neglect of duty, that caused a collision between the 9.02 a.m. GER train from North Woolwich to Fenchurch Street and the 9.22 a.m. LTSR excursion train from Fenchurch Street to Southend. The signalman, noticing that a junction signal approached by the Southend train was giving a false route indication, changed the points in front of the train to correspond with the signal. Although this put the two trains on a collision course, the signalman judged that the train from North Woolwich would clear the junction in time to avoid an accident. Unfortunately this did not happen. The resulting collision derailed the engine and front four carriages of the Southend train and the rear three carriages of the train from North Woolwich. Twenty-nine passengers suffered slight injuries, but there were no fatalities.[30]

A far more serious accident caused by a signalman's error occurred between Finsbury Park (GNR) and Canonbury (NLR) on Saturday 10th December 1881. Shortly after 9 a.m. four NLR trains travelling between Finsbury Park and Broad Street were involved in successive collisions in Canonbury Tunnel. The first train, held by a signal at the south end of the tunnel, was struck in the rear by the second train, but the impact was slight and there were no injuries. The second train was then run into by the third, and very soon afterwards the third was hit by the fourth. A fifth train was stopped just in time at the north end of the tunnel. The relief signalman at Finsbury Park (GNR) had misinterpreted a bell signal received from the signalman at Canonbury Junction (NLR) and had signalled trains forward under a "permissive" arrangement which he should not in any circumstances have employed for loaded passenger trains. Six people were killed and 127 injured, 10 seriously.[31]

29. White p. 80, *Hampstead & Highgate Express* 20.4.1895
30. *London Railway Record* Jan. 2007
31. Robbins pp. 24–25; Young p. 82; Sibley A (ed.), *From Potters Bar to Poplar Dock* (2002) pp. 12–23

RISKS

Shrewd Clerk (with an eye to his percentage). " Take an accident insurance ticket, sir ? "

Passenger (nervously). " Wha' for ? ! "

Clerk. "Well, sir, nothing has gone wrong 'twixt this and London for the last fourteen months; and, by the haverages, the next smash on the hup line is hoverdue exactly six weeks and three days ! ! "

[*Old Gent forks out with alacrity.*

Six weeks after the Canonbury accident, the vicinity of Finsbury Park (GNR) was again the scene of a serious collision. Fog was a very real safety hazard on London's railways, and during the afternoon of Wednesday 25th January 1882 it descended over north London with alarming rapidity and was very dense. Shortly before 5.30 p.m. the driver of the 5.01 p.m. Moorgate Street to Barnet train missed a signal at danger north of Finsbury Park, lost his bearings in the fog, and failed to slow down for the scheduled stop at Hornsey. Travelling at a speed of twenty miles per hour, his train struck the preceding 4.23 p.m. Victoria to Enfield train in the platform of Hornsey Station. Three passengers were killed and sixty-eight injured. The driver of the Barnet train was wholly to blame for the accident.[32]

With gas lighting in railway carriages there was always a risk of gas cylinders igniting in a collision. This is just what happened at Clapham Junction on the evening of Saturday 20th August 1892, when the driver of the 9.50 p.m. Waterloo to Feltham train passed a signal at danger and ran into a train of empty carriages near Ludgate Junction. A gas cylinder under one of the empty carriages ignited and there was a serious fire. An eye witness described it as "a huge conflagration streaming across the huge network of railway lines which divides Battersea in two. ...The flames leaped upwards into the air and cast a lurid glare over the crowds who had gathered round. ...Dark shadows flitted to and fro, and the scene was Rembrandtesque in character". Despite the intensity of the blaze there was only one fatality – the guard of the empty train.

Sunday newspapers carried exaggerated accounts of the collision, and newsboys sold them with cries of "Orful Haccident at the Junction". The sensational press reports may in part have been excused by the spectacular consequences of the accident. The speed with which normal train services were resumed was remarkable by present day standards, but not unusual for the period. There was no complete blockage of traffic through Clapham Junction, and every line was clear within an hour and a half. By seven o'clock on Sunday morning there was no trace of the accident at all.[33]

The derailment of a train at Crystal Palace (LCDR) on Saturday 21st May 1881 must surely have had one of the most bizarre yet poignant consequences of any train accident. As the train from Victoria entered Crystal Palace High Level just before 12.30 p.m., the first and second carriages became derailed, the first falling on its side. There was one fatality – a 12-year-old boy whose body and severed head were found beneath the overturned carriage. It was thought that he had been leaning out of the window at the time of the accident. The lad was recognised by staff at the station as a regular weekend passenger who came to the palace in order to fly his pigeons, but they did not know his name. After the accident no trace of identity could be found, but a bag containing five pigeons was recovered from the overturned carriage. The birds were unharmed, so railway staff tied to a leg of each pigeon a piece of paper conveying the sad news of the boy's death, and released them. Sure enough, a gentleman appeared at the station in less than three hours and declared himself to be the boy's father. The pigeons had flown with their tragic message to the boy's home in Plumstead.[34]

The distressing circumstances of some railway accidents had a profound effect not only on those directly involved but also on the wider community. In the late evening of Saturday 28th January 1882 (just three days after the GNR collision at Hornsey), the NLR suffered a major accident south of Old Ford Station, between Victoria Park and Bow, when a broken drawbar on a northbound goods train caused the derailment of several wagons, obstructing the opposite line. A southbound passenger train which had just left Old Ford

32. *Edmonton Hundred Historical Society Chronicle* Feb.1981
33. *BST* 27.8.1892; *Putney & Wandsworth Borough News* 27.8.1892, 10.9.1892
34. *SLP* 28.5.1881

Station ploughed into the derailed trucks; the engine of the passenger train struck a bridge abutment and the carriages telescoped. Five people lost their lives and twelve were seriously injured.

The reactions of the public and railway staff are noteworthy. On hearing the crash, residents of nearby houses rushed out, leapt over the retaining wall of the cutting in which the accident had occurred, and ran down the line to give assistance. "The night was dark in the cutting and the scene was heart-rending", said one eyewitness. "The broken wood of the carriages and trucks was made into bonfires, the light from which enabled the labourers to carry on their operations." The scene was attended by the locomotive and traffic superintendents of the NLR, and railway officials were commended for being "less reticent than formerly". But the booking clerks at Bow Station, to the south, were criticised for continuing to book passengers after the accident, and allowing them onto an overcrowded platform to wait in vain.

The accident "cast a profound gloom over the whole of the eastern district through which the North London Railway runs, and the locality was, yesterday [Sunday 29th January], visited by many hundreds of people. Feeling allusions were made to the event in some of the churches and chapels at North Bow and Old Ford". A succession of accidents in north and east London had undermined public confidence, prompting this editorial comment in February 1882:

> It has been our lot of late to chronicle more railway disasters on these suburban lines than ever; and the public are really becoming quite timorous when they step into a railway carriage, as to whether they will reach their destinations in safety. The recurrence of such accidents as those at Canonbury, Hornsey and Old Ford will do more to increase the number of empty houses in the suburban districts, very possibly, than the local prevalence of disease or the imposition of high parochial rates.[35]

The speed with which railway companies responded to the lessons learnt from accidents varied considerably. Some changes could be implemented quickly by improvements to the training and supervision of staff, but others required longer-term investment in track, signalling and rolling stock. The cost of compensation claims from passengers could act as a strong incentive, especially after major accidents. Certainly railway companies became less reticent over talking publicly about accidents towards the end of the century, and this greater openness must itself have acted as a stimulus to change.

---

35. *Hackney & Kingsland Gazette* 30.1.1882, 1.2.1882

CHAPTER 9

FROM THE CARRIAGE WINDOW

Fact and Fiction

The passenger on London's late Victorian surface railways who cared to look out of the carriage window had a view of the capital denied to users of other forms of transport:

> *The journey between Vauxhall, or Charing Cross, and Cannon Street, presents to the contemplative man scenes of London life of the most striking description. He is admitted behind the scenes of the poorest neighbourhoods; surveys interminable terraces of back gardens alive with women and children; has a bird's-eye view of potteries and work-yards of many kinds; and, on all sides, from hundreds of fissures and corners, finds his imagination quickened by the feathering of all-compassing steam.*[1]

To Sherlock Holmes, travelling with Dr. Watson through Clapham Junction, the endless terraces and backyards were but the setting for something greater:

> *Holmes was sunk in profound thought, and hardly opened his mouth until we had passed Clapham Junction.*
>
> *"It's a very cheering thing to come into London by any of these lines which run high and allow you to look down upon the houses like this."*
>
> *I thought he was joking, for the view was sordid enough, but he soon explained himself.*
>
> *"Look at those big, isolated clumps of building rising up above the slates, like brick islands in a lead-coloured sea."*
>
> *"The Board schools."*

---

1.   Jerrold B & Doré G, *London: A Pilgrimage* (1872, reprinted 2005) pp. 134–135

"Lighthouses, my boy! Beacons of the future! Capsules, with hundreds of bright little seeds in each, out of which will spring the wiser, better England of the future."[2]

"THE VIEW WAS SORDID ENOUGH."

Observations of late Victorian London as seen from the railway carriage are uncommon, as are first-hand accounts of the train journeys themselves. Yet a few journeys, ordinary enough at the time, have been recorded. Five of them are recalled here – four from the 1870s, the fifth, mixing fact and fiction, from the 1890s.

Outer Circle, 1876

The half-hourly LNWR service from Mansion House to Broad Street had been operating for four years when this journey was made. The booking clerk at Mansion House expresses mild surprise when asked for a ticket to Broad Street (less than a mile distant by road from Mansion House), but the first class ticket is duly issued at a fare of one shilling and threepence. The white and brown carriages of the LNWR train are crowded, nearly every compartment being full. But at Blackfriars about half the passengers leave the train and a

---

2.   Doyle A Conan, *The Memoirs of Sherlock Holmes: The Adventure of the Naval Treaty* (*Strand Magazine* 1893) p. 130

similar number join it. This pattern is repeated at most stations to Victoria, where the train becomes less crowded.

At Gloucester Road Station the guard makes his way from carriage to carriage checking tickets. "It looks as if he, too, has not often the pleasure of beholding travellers who go with him all the way from the Mansion House to Broad Street, for, after glancing at the ticket indicating the journey, he gives a wink at the ticket-holder indicating great inward satisfaction. So easy it is to make a man happy."

Beyond Earl's Court the train leaves its subterranean route and runs level with fields and gardens. Kensington Addison Road Station proves to be "a quite unique piece of railway architecture":

> It must be one of the airiest, if not the airiest, station in the kingdom. The model of the builder was clearly a worn-out umbrella, with a few good-sized holes in the top. The huge place is covered in, partly but not entirely, by a glass roof, while the sides are perfectly open, allowing the freest ingress to the winds of heaven.

The train now enters what had been, until recently, open country, but is no more:

> A glimpse from the carriage window, as the train is gliding along through the sunlit fields between Kensington Station and Shepherd's Bush, gives one a very good idea as to how the growth of that monster, London, is taking place. There are a few houses here and a few there, in solitary groups, looking as if dropped from a balloon upon the grass-grown land.

The larger building forming the nucleus of the whole is the public house, and a few shops are beginning to appear.

Beyond Uxbridge Road Station there are still green fields, and at Wormwood Scrubs passengers are scarce. On arrival at Willesden Junction the train again begins to fill:

> The remaining part of the circular tour is the most pleasant, through being entirely above ground... over a line carried in great part upon arches, and thus giving a good view of the surrounding country. It is charming for the first four or five miles after leaving Willesden Junction, with the northern hills of London, Hampstead, and Highgate, in the foreground, and to right and left pleasant fields, dotted over in all directions with villa residences surrounded by gardens.

At Gospel Oak "we are now entering the north-westerly fringe of the great metropolis, flying along over the roofs of houses and over streets that are getting more and more full of life as we advance".

A great crowd, as large as any on the earlier, underground section, awaits the train at Camden Town:

> ...thenceforth at each succeeding station, Barnsbury, Islington, Canonbury, Dalston, and Haggerston, the movement is incessant, the large platforms – contrasting strongly, both in size and comfort... with the necessarily cramped stations on the Metropolitan lines – being nearly all filled with arriving passengers.

Broad Street is reached punctually one hour and nine minutes after leaving Mansion House. The journey, through twenty-seven stations, has been made at a fare of about a halfpenny a mile. The ticket collector at Broad Street calls out to his colleague:

> "I say, Jack, one has come all the way from the Mansion House by this 'ere train. Did you ever?"

To which Jack responds:

> "I never! P'raps he meant to take a short cut."

Our passenger leaves the station to a chorus of boisterous laughter.[3]

Ally Pally, 1876

The second Alexandra Palace, built after the first was burnt down, had been open just a year when this journey was made by GNR train from King's Cross. The ride, on a sunny day, is described as being "like a flight from pandemonium to paradise", a dismal start giving way to a charming finish. "The moment the train has left the large and somewhat dark terminus of King's Cross it is in the bowels of a tunnel black as Erebus." Between the first tunnel and the second a glimpse of sunshine "only serves to light up the heavy walls of a mortuary, standing on the embankment overhanging the railway":

> The sight of it seems to inspire an oily blackcoated man in our compartment, apparently an undertaker, to give a lady next to him some particulars of the Great Northern steam apparatus for burying people. A daily train, says he, cheerfully rubbing his cotton-gloved hands, carries "a load of dead" down to the neighbourhood of Colney Hatch, where there is the healthiest cemetery to be found anywhere near London.

---

3.   *RFS* July 1876 quoting *Railway News*

From Holloway the tracks spread out widely, the mass of lines, carried on arches above the housetops, continuing to Finsbury Park. This station is exposed and draughty, but "in compensation there are pleasant views to be obtained from the platform over the adjoining flowery ground of Finsbury Park". After passing above the MR Tottenham and Hampstead line and through Crouch End Station, the train enters "one of the most lovely valleys to be found anywhere near London":

> It is sheltered on two sides by woods and coppices, while the open parts, to the east and south, allow a wide range of view over undulating fields and corn lands, with here and there a silvery streak of river shining out in the distance.

Beyond Highgate and its tunnels the train enters an area of woodland, predominantly evergreen:

> The last mile of the line from King's Cross to the Alexandra Park is perhaps the prettiest mile of railway scenery to be found so close to the metropolis. There is an immense panorama lying outstretched before the eye, the view embracing four or five counties, bounded only by the hazy blue of the plains of Herts and Essex, and the dark grey canopy of smoke that everlastingly crowns the head of our modern Babylon.[4]

Down to the Docks, 1877

The railway from Stratford to North Woolwich had been open thirty years when this journey was made, but through trains to North Woolwich from the new Liverpool Street terminus had been running for only three years. Despite its new rolling stock, the line is here portrayed as a less than efficient backwater of the GER.

Our passenger, intending to travel from Liverpool Street to Custom House, finds that even the new GER terminus suffers from poor gas lighting: "Hold your little one tighter by the hand and tell him not to be frightened for it is not a tomb but the great station Liverpool Street":

> Having taken our tickets we proceed up a platform to a train composed of new carriages and pervaded by a smell of newness. After sitting there some few minutes, during which time our only recreation is that man with his cries of "Woo'ch Train", there is a violent banging of doors, a whistle and off we go.

---

4.   *RFS* May 1876 quoting *Railway News*

The first station, Bishopsgate, "bears a most dismal aspect". Bethnal Green, however, "is absolutely better lighted, or it appears so, than its mother station". Delays then occur, and Stratford Bridge [soon to be renamed Stratford Market] is reached ten minutes late. This station attracts a note of sarcasm:

> *...put your head out of the window and look at the station but shade your eyes for fear the dazzling splendour irritates them – a magnificent building meets your view – of one storey high joined to the other side of the line by a wooden structure – draw in your head again and stifle that belief of the building being a relic of the middle ages.*

At Canning Town the train overshoots the platform – "all the better for the passengers living in the middle of Victoria Dock Road" – but it reverses back into the station. At Tidal Basin our reporter's carriage again stops where there is no platform:

> *I find there's some distance to jump from the carriage to the ground but heartily sick and disgusted I perform the sailor-like operation and walk away.*

The final stage of the journey to Custom House is just too much for him![5]

Midland Roundabout, 1878

The MR service from St. Pancras to Earl's Court via Child's Hill, Acton and Hammersmith was short-lived, running only from 1878 to 1880. So we are fortunate to have a first-hand account of a journey on this service as it makes its wide circuit round north-west and west London:

> *...taking one of the fifteen trains per day of the new service, we found it, without surprise, admirably equipped, the train being made up of first and third class carriages... the Midland thirds being really excellent seconds, with stuffed seats, parcel and hat racks, plate glass in the sliding frames of the doors and the elbow lights.*

The first part of the journey from St. Pancras passes coal sidings, cattle pens and the retaining walls of cuttings. The NLR crosses overhead near Camden Road, the Hampstead Junction Line near Haverstock Hill and again at Finchley Road. At Child's Hill and Cricklewood the train forks left onto the Midland and South Western Junction Line. At Dudding Hill the line "runs through a very charming district, hybrid, rural, and suburban, many fine pasture fields in one direction, and in another direction new houses of various classes, some of them very picturesque, either very recently finished or in progress" – then

5.   *Courier & East London Advertiser* 4.5.1877

on through Harrow Road and over the LNWR and GWR main lines to Acton "with its pleasant surroundings".

The train turns south and east, reaching Turnham Green "with its numerous parties of cricketers in full play", then runs through "a rich market garden district" to Shaftesbury Road. From here the new direct line to Hammersmith is followed (opened 1877), then the MDR extension line of 1874 through West Kensington to Earl's Court. For passengers continuing eastward, an MDR train to Mansion House arrives at Earl's Court within three minutes:

> *Here, during this short interval, we had more than a glimpse of the busy traffic done on the District line by the London and North Western, the Midland, the District, and other companies, well-filled trains following each other in each direction, with amazing rapidity.*[6]

"Express" to Ludgate Hill, 1892

The final railway journey recorded here combines fact and fiction. The route by LCDR limited stop train from Clapham Junction to Ludgate Hill is real enough, but this forms the background to a short story for Christmas published in the *Brixton and Streatham Times* on 24th December 1892 under the title "That Express".

The express in question was scheduled to run non-stop from Loughborough Junction to Ludgate Hill. But these expresses, observed the writer, had a habit of stopping between the stations at which ordinary trains called, "and if they get over the bridge at Blackfriars without affording their unfortunate passengers a prolonged opportunity for examining the beauties of the silvery Thames, it may be reckoned with confidence that something has gone wrong with the works".

The storyteller, a journalist, found himself alone in a third class compartment of the express on Christmas Eve. During the journey from Clapham Junction to Ludgate Hill he planned to put the finishing touches to an article, despite the fact that

> *...a Chatham and Dover third class carriage is about the worst thing you could possibly select for such a purpose. Light? The flickering oil lamps do little more than make darkness visible, and as for comfort – well, the inside of a Wandsworth Road 'bus what time the driver is trying to get in front of a tramcar could hardly be better fitted for turning the milk of human kindness into rancid butter.*

Facing up to these discomforts, and the hardness of the wooden seat, the journalist lit his pipe and began to write.

He glanced out of the window as Wandsworth Road, Clapham and Brixton were passed, and "all looked well for an undisturbed and pleasant ride to Ludgate Hill". But at

---

6.   *RSOG* June 1878 quoting *Railway News*

Loughborough Junction, just after the guard had given the "right away", a lady, pursued by two men, rushed onto the platform. With the help of a porter the lady was bundled into the journalist's compartment, whilst the two men, evidently against their will, were hustled into another compartment nearby. The journalist took stock of his new travelling companion – a pleasant-looking woman of about twenty-five with a fresh and bright young face and dark, expressive eyes beneath a mass of dark, wavy hair. She spoke first:

> *"Can you tell me how long we shall be before we reach the City?"*
> *"With good fortune we might expect to reach Ludgate Hill in about*
> *a quarter of an hour."*
> *"Do we stop at any of the other stations?"*
> *"Oh no, this is an express to the City."*
> *"Then you have just fifteen minutes in which to make up your mind…*
> *whether you will marry me tomorrow morning, or—"*

The journalist caught a glimpse of the platforms at Elephant and Castle as the train rushed through; he then caught a glimpse of a long, slender hat pin that the lady had produced:

> *Just as we dashed through Borough Road my lady made a sudden rush*
> *over to my corner, scattered my precious MSS to the winds, and raising*
> *her weapon on high, declared that if I did not give my consent at once she*
> *would bury it in my craven heart. It was an exciting position.*

Would the train stop, as it so often did, on Blackfriars Bridge? "My heart almost ceased to beat as we dashed onto the bridge. On, on and on…" The express rattled unchecked across the bridge. "Just as my senses were leaving me and my travelling companion had made ready for the fatal stroke" the train steamed into Ludgate Hill. As soon as it had stopped the two men who had boarded at Loughborough Junction flung open the door of the compartment, seized the woman, and hurried her off without a word.

A subsequent newspaper report read:

> *Mrs. Louisa Manning, who stands accused of having murdered her husband*
> *and two children under circumstances of a horrible character, was removed*
> *from Wandsworth Prison to Newgate, in readiness for the opening of the*
> *Central Criminal Court. Mrs. Manning, who is believed to be insane,*
> *was in the care of two experienced warders, and travelled by train from*
> *Clapham Junction.*[7]

Where better for this drama to unfold than in the smoke-laden gloom of the Metropolitan Extension Line on a late Victorian Christmas Eve?

---

7.   *BST* 24.12.1892

INDEX